The Dyscalculia Toolkit:
Supporting Learning Difficulties in Maths

The Dyscalculia Toolkit:
Supporting Learning Difficulties in Maths

Ronit Bird

Los Angeles | London | New Delhi
Singapore | Washington DC

First published 2007

Reprinted 2009

SAGE Publications Ltd
1 Oliver's Yard
55 City Road
London EC1Y 1SP

SAGE Publications Inc.
2455 Teller Road
Thousand Oaks, California 91320

SAGE Publications India Pvt Ltd
B 1/I 1 Mohan Cooperative Industrial Area
Mathura Road
New Delhi 110 044

SAGE Publications Asia-Pacific Pte Ltd
33 Pekin Street #02-01
Far East Square
Singapore 048763

Library of Congress Control Number: 2007935605

A catalogue record for this book is available from the British Library

ISBN 978-1-4129-4764-0
ISBN 978-1-4129-4765-7 (pbk)

Typeset by Pantek Arts Ltd, Maidstone, Kent
Printed in Great Britain by CPI Antony Rowe, Chippenham, Wiltshire
Printed on paper from sustainable resources

FSC
Mixed Sources
Product group from well-managed forests and other controlled sources
Cert no. SGS-COC-2953
www.fsc.org
© 1996 Forest Stewardship Council

Contents

Introduction

How to use this book   xv

Dysclaculia and other specific learning difficulties   xvii

Section 1: EARLY NUMBER WORK – NUMBERS UP TO 10

Overview   1

What are the main problems?   2

How to help   2

Activities and games:

    Activity – Make dot patterns for the numbers 1 to 10   3

    Game – Make 5   4

    Activities – Become familiar with Cuisenaire rods   5

    Activity – Explore odd and even with Cuisenaire rods and with money   7

    Game – Odd and Even Collectors   8

    Game – Draw Your Race on a Number Line   9

    Activities – Use Cuisenaire rods to learn all components of the numbers 1–10   10

    Activity – Make and read equations with Cuisenaire rods   11

    Activities – Draw and record equations in writing   12

    Activity – Make up word problems to match a given number fact   13

    Game – Cover the Numbers, or Shut the Box   14

    Game – Clear the Deck   15

    Activity – Make a bead string, in two colours, of 10 beads   16

    Activity – Learn complements of 10 with the bead string   17

    Game – How Many Beads? How Many Are Hidden?   18

    Activity – Find complements of 10 with Cuisenaire rods   18

    Game – Complements Number Search   19

    Game – Complements Ping-Pong   20

    Game – Ten in a Bed   21

    Activities – Explore and learn the doubles up to 5 + 5   22

    Activities – Estimate and measure using Cuisenaire rods   24

    Activities – Focus on plus/minus 1 and plus/minus 2   26

    Game – Who Has the Most Equations?   27

    Activity – Compare the difference and equalise   28

    Activities – Hidden quantity subtraction   29

Activity – Teach complementary addition   30

Activity – Complementary addition on a number line   31

Activity – Use reasoning to find near-complements and near-doubles   32

Activity – Identify which strategy works best in different situations   32

Activities – Use money for component work   33

Section 2: BASIC CALCULATION WITH NUMBERS ABOVE 10

Overview   35

What are the main problems?   35

How to help   36

Activities and games:

Activity – Connect the numbers 10–20 with the numbers below 10   37

Activities – Focus on the 'teen' numbers   38

Activities – Explore the numbers between 10 and 20 with Cuisenaire rods   40

Activities – Locate two-digit numbers and put them in context   42

Activities – Complements to 20   44

Activity – Complements to larger multiples of 10   46

Activity – Complements on a number line   47

Activity – Introduce bridging through 10 with Cuisenaire rods   47

Games – Five and What's Left   48

Activity – Bridge through 10 on a number line   49

Activity – Practise bridging and reinforce the commutativity of addition   50

Activity – Bridge through multiples of 10 on a number line   51

Game – Race along a Number Line and Bridge   51

Game – Race to the End of the Number Line   52

Activity – Complementary addition, or subtraction by adding   53

Activity – Complementary addition for subtracting round numbers   54

Activity – Harder complementary addition on a number line   56

Activity – A flexible approach to partitioning   57

Activities – Explore partitioning methods for two-digit mental additions   57

Activity – Teach an alternative written method for column addition   58

Activity – Show how to avoid decomposition in subtraction   59

Activities – Complements to 100   59

Game – Keep the Change!   62

Activity – Learn the doubles up to 10 + 10   62

Activities – Practise and extend the doubles facts   63

Activity – Halving is the opposite of doubling   64

Activity – Find half of round numbers   65

Activity – Function machines for doubling and halving   65

Activity – Use reasoning to find near-complements and near-doubles   66

Activity – 9 is almost 10   67

Activity – The Basic 8 strategies   68

Activity – Identify which strategy works best in different situations   69

Section 3: PLACE VALUE

Overview   71

What are the main problems?   71

How to help   72

Activities and games:

Activities – Exchange units into tens   73

Activities – Concrete counting on place value mats   73

Game – Magic 10s   75

Activities – Make a 20-step staircase and explore the 'teen' number names   75

Activity – Cover 20   76

Game – Race to Cover 100   76

Game – Four Throws to Reach 100   77

Activities – Make and read numbers made of Cuisenaire rods or base-10 materials   78

Games – Dice and spinner games   79

Activities – Practise subtraction and decomposition with concrete materials   80

Game – Spot the Decomposition   81

Activities – Use a spike abacus   82

Game – Win Counters on a 100-Square   83

Game – Race through a 100-Square   84

Activities – Practise adding and subtracting 10 and 100   85

Game – Steer the Number   85

Activity – Transform a two-digit number in two steps   86

Activity – Teach the threefold repeating pattern: units, tens and hundreds   87

Activities – Explore place value as a shorthand   87

Activities – Read and write multi-digit numbers   88

Activities – Build up large numbers, one column at a time   89

Activity – What is the value of . . .   89

Game – Two-Digit Sequences   91

Game – Three-Digit Sequences with the Focus on Tens   92

Game – Place Value Boxes   93

Game – Calculator Skittles   94

Activity – Partition numbers into tens and units in various ways   95

Activity – Split off the 'teen' numbers   95

Game – Jump 10   96

Activities – Locate any number on a number line   97

Game – The Six-Card Rounding Game   98

Game – The Rounding Challenge   98

Activity – Teach $\times$ 10 and $\div$ 10 as a shift between columns   99

Activity – Extend place value thinking to decimals   100

Activity – Connect decimal place value notation to money   101

Section 4: TIMES TABLES, MULTIPLICATION AND DIVISION

Overview   103

What are the main problems?   103

How to help   104

Activities and games:

Activities – Build small numbers out of equal-sized groups   105

Activity – Connect division to multiplication from the very beginning   106

Activity – Illustrate simple word problems   107

Activity – Use Cuisenaire rods to show that multiplication is commutative   107

Activities – Use Cuisenaire rods to connect multiplication and division   109

Activity – Connect step-counting (repeated addition) with multiplication   110

Activity – Step-count one or two steps from various tables facts   111

Activity – practise mental step-counting from given tables facts   113

Activities – Make times tables patterns on a 100-square   114

Activities – Make times tables patterns on number lines   115

Activities – Double means 'multiply by 2'   116

Activity – $\times$ 5 is half of $\times$ 10   116

Activity – Find all the steps of any times table by reasoning from key facts   117

Activity – $\times$ 9 is almost $\times$ 10   119

Games to practise individual times tables using self-correcting cards   119

Game – Don't Walk if You Can Take the Bus   120

Game – The Mouse Tables Game   122

Activity – Construct a multiplication grid   124

Activity – Complete a partially-filled multiplication grid   126

Game – Multiples from the 1–6 Times Tables   127

Activity – Harder mixed tables practice 128

Game – Factors 128

Activity – Diagrammatic practice of the area model of multiplication 130

Activity – Use rectangle sketches to help derive new multiplication facts 130

Activities – Change the shape of the multiplication rectangle 131

Game – Areas on a Grid 133

Suggestions for Further Reading 135

Index 137

Author's biographical details

Ronit Bird is a teacher whose interest in pupils with specific learning difficulties began with a focus on dyslexia. She qualified as a teacher at London University and subsequently gained a further qualification as a specialist teacher. While working with dyslexic pupils in a mainstream school, Ronit started to develop strategies and teaching activities to help support the learning of pupils who were experiencing difficulties in Maths.

Ronit has taught in both primary and secondary settings, and has worked as a SENCO in both the independent and state sectors. She currently works as a teacher and as a contributor to professional development courses for teachers on dyscalculia. Ronit is also currently involved in the Harrow Dyscalculia Project.

CD

The CD accompanying this book contains a large number of resources, allowing teachers to put together a tailor-made package of suitable activities from different sections of the book for particular pupils or groups.

You will find on the CD an introduction to concrete manipulative materials and Cuisenaire rods in the Appendix, and a further 29 pages of resources, including some worksheets and all the necessary game-boards for the games mentioned in the text.

Contents of the CD

Appendix: An introduction to concrete manipulative materials and Cuisenaire rods

Copiable resources on the CD

Some things you can do with your Cuisenaire rods

Dot pattern cards and box

Make 5 game board

Draw Your Race on a Number Line game board

Cover the Numbers (or Shut the Box) game board

Ten in a Bed game board rules

Compare the difference and equalise activity sheet

Which strategy? worksheet

Five and What's Left Game, and Three and What's Left game boards

Race along a Number Line and Bridge game board

Race to the End of the Line game board

Complements to 100 worksheet

Money – how much change? activity sheet

Double and half worksheet

Reasoning from complements facts worksheet

Reasoning from doubles facts worksheet

Cards for the Basic 8 mental arithmetic strategies

Place value mats

Nets for making shallow trays for work with Cuisenaire rods

The Four Throws game board

100-squares, arranged horizontally and vertically

Add 10, a place value activity sheet

Subtract 10, a place value activity sheet

Times tables patterns on a number line blank

The Multiples game board

Rectangles for a worksheet on the area model of multiplication and division

Name the Factors game board

More Factors game board

Introduction

How to use this book

This book is for teachers who are looking for practical ways to help pupils who struggle with maths. It is aimed mainly at primary teachers who do not have a specialist background in either maths or special needs. I hope it will also be of interest to parents, teaching assistants and teachers in SEN departments who support pupils in junior school and in the early years of secondary school.

This book is a collection of teaching activities and games. The activities have been developed over a number of years of teaching dyslexic, dyspraxic and dyscalculic pupils, either on a one-to-one basis or in small groups of pupils who have been withdrawn from lessons for extra support. The activities are equally appropriate for children who have been diagnosed as dyscalculic and for those whose difficulties with number are one of the symptoms of their dyslexia or dyspraxia. Indeed, the suggestions presented here are designed to promote understanding and to help learners make connections, and are therefore suitable for teaching the basic principles of numeracy to any pupil.

The philosophy behind this book is to provide children with the kinds of practical experiences that will help them build sound cognitive models. Because the emphasis is on doing the maths rather than recording it on paper, you will find very few worksheets or ideas for written work in this book. Instead you will find 200 teaching activities and 40 games. I have deliberately included activities that require only what can easily be found in a normal maths classroom or can easily be acquired by parents, such as counters, Cuisenaire rods, Dienes blocks, number cards, dice, paper and pencils. There is no need to buy special equipment, or commercial games and resources that tend to target only a single topic. The activities are simple to set up and most are ready for immediate use with individual pupils or small groups; others just require copies of the games boards or activity sheets that you can find on the CD.

The book is organised into four sections:

1 Early number work – numbers up to 10

2 Basic calculation with numbers above 10

3 Place value

4 Times tables, multiplication and division.

Resources for all four sections can be found on the CD attached to the book.

I have targeted what I know to be specific areas of difficulty and have deliberately broken down the teaching and learning into very small steps. Each section is loosely structured in order of difficulty, starting with concrete activities and progressing gradually through learning activities that are designed to help pupils move through the intermediate diagrammatic stage and right up to the abstract stage of calculation.

Most of the activities are designed to be teacher-led, rather than for children to work through on their own. It is important to ask lots of questions, to direct the discussion carefully, to point out any connections with previous activities and other maths topics, and to encourage pupils to talk a lot about what they are doing, and why, while they are doing it. Naturally, pupils will do best in an atmosphere where mistakes are regarded as a normal, and even an instructive, part of the learning process.

I regard the activities and games in this book as absolutely central to the teaching of pupils who have difficulties with basic maths. Enjoyable as they may be, they should not be seen as just a bit of fun to fill in the spare time at the end of a lesson. They are carefully designed to provide the actual learning experience for a variety of specific maths topics.

Please do not feel that you ought to start at the beginning of the book and work through to the end, or even to keep to the sequence in which the ideas are presented. Instead, you should feel free to pick and choose activities, depending on your pupils and on your knowledge of their particular areas of difficulty. Some activities may need to be repeated often, or revisited at regular intervals; others may be valuable to try only once for particular pupils or not at all. When activities naturally follow on from each other, the text clearly signals the fact. Some activities may need to be preceded by others from another section; for example, some understanding of place value (Section 3) is required before attempting some of the work on larger numbers (Section 2) and before some of the work on multiplication and division (Section 4). Once you begin working closely with pupils, you will find that you are the person best placed to uncover any misconceptions or sticking points that could usefully become the focus of subsequent lessons.

Each section starts with a short overview, putting the topic of that section into context. Following the overview, you will find a summary of the main problems associated with the topic and ideas on how to help. These summaries are presented as bullet points for ease of reference. The remainder of each section is dedicated entirely to the teaching activities and games, set out as clearly and concisely as possible with a minimum of explanatory background or theory. The 200 activities are labelled according to the main teaching point they have been designed to address. A list of teaching points is also included in the instructions for each of the 40 games. Printable and photocopiable resources are provided on the CD, 💿 making the activities and games accessible and ready to use, with the minimum of preparation.

The Appendix contains a summary of the more commonly used concrete materials, including an introduction to Cuisenaire rods. Because I use Cuisenaire rods so extensively in my teaching activities, and have found so many people unfamiliar with their use, I have also included on the CD 💿 a leaflet of practical ideas, written originally for parents. The leaflet is sized so as to fit inside a box of Cuisenaire rods.

I use the word 'teacher' loosely in this book to mean anyone who supports children in their learning, including, of course, teaching assistants and parents. Indeed, parents are ideally placed to use the ideas in this book to promote maths as a practical subject full of patterns and puzzles and therefore full of interest and fun. Whether inside the classroom or at home, the best results will be achieved by frequent, regular, short, but unhurried, sessions, each of which should include a variety of activities and topics and a sensitive balance between revision and new content. Daily sessions will soon improve pupils' attitude and will steadily boost their self-assurance, their sense of achievement and their maths performance.

DYSCALCULIA AND OTHER SPECIFIC LEARNING DIFFICULTIES

Developmental dyscalculia was first recognised by the Department for Education and Skills (2001) and defined (p. 2) as:

> *a condition that affects the ability to acquire arithmetical skills. Dyscalculic learners may have difficulty understanding simple number concepts, lack an intuitive grasp of numbers, and have problems learning number facts and procedures. Even if they produce a correct answer or use a correct method, they may do so mechanically and without confidence.*

There is a debate about whether true dyscalculia differs from the maths difficulties experienced by some dyslexic and dyspraxic learners, a debate I am happy to leave to the academics. What matters to me is the fact that the same sorts of intervention seem to help many pupils who are underachieving in maths, whatever label they have been given. I believe that the coming years will see a growing recognition of the particular problems and educational needs of dyscalculic learners, in much the same way as the last two decades have seen an increasing acceptance of the existence of dyslexia and a developing consensus about the best teaching and learning approaches for these pupils.

As a teacher, you might suspect that you have a dyscalculic pupil in your class if an otherwise competent student has a surprising level of difficulty with ordinary numeric operations and relies on finger-counting, often for all four arithmetic operations, well beyond the age at which most of the others in the class have progressed to more efficient strategies. A dyscalculic learner stands out as having no 'feel for numbers' at all, no ability to estimate even small quantities, and no idea whether an answer to an arithmetic problem is reasonable or not. Memory weaknesses, both long-term and short-term, are a great handicap and result in a pupil with dyscalculia being unable to remember facts and procedures accurately, or consistently, no matter how many times they try to learn them by heart. Pupils who have dyscalculia simply cannot remember their times tables reliably, and you may find they can recall some facts one day but not the next. They are also likely to lose track of what they are doing when attempting any procedure that requires more than two or three steps. Even basic counting can be a problem for pupils with dyscalculia, especially counting backwards.

Indicators for dyscalculia are:

◆ an inability to subitise (see without counting) even very small quantities

◆ an inability to estimate whether a numerical answer is reasonable

◆ weaknesses in both short-term and long-term memory

◆ an inability to count backwards reliably

◆ a weakness in visual and spatial orientation

◆ directional (left/right) confusion

◆ slow processing speeds when engaged in maths activities

◆ trouble with sequencing

◆ a tendency not to notice patterns

◆ a problem with all aspects of money

◆ a marked delay in learning to read a clock to tell the time

◆ an inability to manage time in their daily lives.

Research into dyscalculia is still at an early stage, but it is estimated that dyscalculia affects roughly 4–6% of the population. This equates to at least one child in any average classroom.

A dyslexic pupil might show many of the same indicators as those mentioned above, because it is thought that at least half of all dyslexics also have difficulties with maths. Outside the maths classroom, you might suspect that pupils are dyslexic if they read and write much less willingly and fluently than you might expect, if they read and reread written material with little comprehension and if their spelling is particularly weak, inconsistent or bizarre. Dyslexic learners show much greater ability and understanding when speaking than you could ever guess from looking at the scrappy and minimal amount of written work they produce. Other indicators are memory weaknesses, problems with processing auditory information, and difficulties with planning and organisation.

A typical dyspraxic pupil does not seem to have the same long-term memory problems as a dyslexic and so might be able to remember times-tables facts with ease. Dyspraxia, also known as developmental coordination disorder, mainly affects motor control, which results in pupils being clumsy and uncoordinated, poor at planning and organisation, and unsuccessful at subjects such as PE and sports that require balance and coordination. Dyspraxic pupils cannot process sensory information properly and are therefore forever tripping and falling, dropping and breaking things, and mislaying their belongings. In the maths classroom, dyspraxic pupils have particular difficulty handling equipment such as a ruler, a protractor or a set of compasses, and their written work is likely to be very messy and difficult to decipher.

A pupil with attention deficit hyperactivity disorder (ADHD), may signal his (and it is usually a boy) presence by being unable to stop fidgeting or to sit still, being too easily distracted by outside stimuli, having a tendency to talk and interrupt excessively, and finding it extremely difficult to stay on task and see any undertaking through to the end. I mention the condition here only because nowadays pupils with ADHD or ADD come under the umbrella term of 'pupils with specific difficulties'. However, pupils with attention disorders may not have any specific problems with maths once they have found a way to manage their impulsivity and concentration difficulties.

SECTION 1

Early number work – numbers up to 10

Overview

This first section deals with very small numbers, but not necessarily with very small children. Older pupils often have difficulties that can be traced back to misconceptions at this very early stage.

Early number work depends on counting. But some children have difficulty with counting. For example, dyspraxic children can find it very challenging to coordinate a one-to-one correspondence between the numbers they learn to recite and the objects they wish to count. Their counting is, therefore, often inaccurate. Some children learn to chant the string of numbers as if they were the words to a nursery rhyme, without really understanding what they mean.

Pupils who experience difficulties with maths know that they are weak in this area and feel that they cannot trust their own memory about even the most basic of number facts. This leads to a reliance on counting on their fingers, in ones. The problem is that counting in ones is a very inefficient strategy. Every step provides another opportunity for mistakes to creep in. Furthermore, it puts an unnecessary strain on working memory, because calculating by counting involves a double-counting process: not only must children keep track of the running total, they must also keep a separate, parallel count of how much they are adding or subtracting so that they will know when to stop the reckoning. Another persistent problem for dyscalculic pupils is an uncertainty about where to start any count, because they are not sure whether they are supposed to be counting actual numbers or the intervals between numbers. Any new fact that is arrived at only after so much effort, anxiety and time is unlikely to be stored in long-term memory, and so a vicious cycle begins.

One of the best ways to help pupils with specific maths difficulties is to use the right kinds of apparatus to provide mathematical models that can be explored, understood and internalised. Concrete, manipulative materials can help give pupils a stronger number sense and can teach pupils how to see numbers in relation to each other. The Appendix 💿 gives an introduction to concrete materials, and in particular to Cuisenaire rods, which are used extensively in the activities in this book.

What are the main problems?

◆ Reciting the string of numbers without understanding what counting really means.

◆ Not appreciating the concept of cardinality, i.e. that the final number of the count *is* the quantity of the set.

◆ Being unaware of patterns, e.g. the fact that larger numbers contain smaller numbers.

◆ Being unable to recall simple number facts and number bonds reliably.

◆ Feeling constantly muddled about whether adding involves counting numbers, or the steps (intervals) between numbers.

◆ Counting in ones, with each unnecessary step providing an opportunity to make a mistake.

◆ Using such inefficient calculation methods that number facts cannot lodge in long-term memory.

How to help

◆ Give pupils plenty of time at the early stages before moving on. Revisit basic activities often.

◆ Use appropriate concrete materials that will help build cognitive models.

◆ Let the pupils manipulate the concrete materials. Do not monopolise them yourself or use them only for demonstrations.

◆ Start by doing something concretely, before recording the maths in writing. Too often the reverse occurs, when manipulatives are used only to illustrate what a written calculation means.

◆ Bear in mind that work with concrete materials should come before diagrams, and that pictures and diagrams are the transitional stage between concrete and abstract work.

◆ Be explicit about what is happening at every step. Ask questions and encourage a lot of talk.

◆ Set up lots of opportunities to count, beginning at different starting points. Use actual objects for counting, especially for counting backwards, before progressing to more abstract counting.

◆ Give plenty of experience in exploring the individual numbers up to 10. Use both discrete and continuous concrete materials: counters, bead strings and Cuisenaire rods.

◆ Play games that actually teach the points you want the pupils to learn. Ten such games and more than 50 targeted activities are detailed in this section. Send games home for homework sometimes instead of worksheets.

◆ Teach component work in a way that reinforces the connection between adding and subtracting.

◆ Break topics down into the smallest of steps, e.g. teach plus or minus 1 before plus or minus 2.

◆ Guide pupils to see that it is more efficient to start from the larger number when counting on.

◆ Minimise the number of facts that have to be known by heart.

◆ Minimise the number of strategies that a pupil must know. Even if you demonstrate or explain several different strategies, allow each pupil to choose only one or two to practise.

◆ Teach explicitly how to reason from known or given facts.

◆ Vary the mathematical vocabulary, e.g. use 'subtract', 'less than', 'decrease' or 'minus', as well as 'take away'.

◆ Show pupils how to identify what kinds of problems can be solved by each new strategy.

◆ Locate number problems in real situations that have meaning for the pupil, e.g. 'two more toys' rather than the abstract 'two more', or the unimaginable 'two more metres per second'.

◆ Allow informal jottings before teaching standard written notation.

◆ Have pupils make up their own number problems and their own word problems.

 Activity

Make dot patterns for the numbers 1 to 10

Give pupils a pile of chunky, attractive and easy-to-handle objects such as glass nuggets, plastic counters or buttons. The objects should be of roughly the same size and colour as each other. Let pupils practise making and reading dot patterns for all the numbers from 1 to 10. The patterns for the first six numbers are those found on dice, with which most children are already familiar. If they do not recognise these patterns, encourage the children to play lots of board games with dice at home. The numbers 7–10 are not standardised in the same way. I like to use the patterns proposed by Dorian Yeo in her 2003 book *Dyslexia, Dyspraxia & Mathematics*. Unlike most of the patterns found on playing card and dominos, Yeo's patterns are based on doubles and near-doubles and therefore illustrate a key fact about each number, from which other facts can be derived. For example, a child who 'sees' the number 8 as two groups of 4 can readily 'calculate' that 8 – 4 = 4 or that 4 + 5 must be 9.

After inviting a child to make the dot pattern for a particular number, e.g. the number 9, ask as varied a set of questions as you can about the key components. Start with more descriptive language before making your question purely abstract. For example: *What must you add to the pattern of 5 if you want to make 9? If we take away the pattern of 5 from the pattern of 9, what is left? If I have a pattern of 5 and you have a pattern of 9, how many more dots do you have than I have? I have 5 and you have 9, so how much more than me do you have? 4 and 5 more is what? 4 and what number makes 9? 4 add what is 9?* Next, hide the pattern and ask the same kinds of questions.

At later sessions give pupils squared paper on which to make the dot patterns using small round stickers. Keep these activities going, using both concrete and diagrammatic representations, until pupils can answer any kind of question about the key facts, i.e. the double or near-double facts, for all the numbers up to 10 without hesitation and without having to make or see the number patterns first.

Dot patterns for making cards can be found on the CD at the back of this book. Activities to help children learn the dot patterns are given in Yeo's book, *Dyslexia, Dyspraxia & Mathematics*. Three of her ideas for games are summarised on the back of the cut-out card box that is provided together with the dot pattern cards on the CD.

Game
Make 5

A game for two players.

Teaching points:

◆ The game teaches children to split and recombine small numbers up to 5.

◆ It teaches that larger numbers contain smaller numbers within them.

◆ It teaches that there are only two different ways to build 5 from whole numbers: 1 + 4 or 2 + 3.

◆ It teaches the commutative property of addition, i.e. that 1 + 4 is equal to 4 + 1.

Equipment needed:

◆ A game board for each player (see CD).

◆ A pack of 17 cards, made up of four cards each of the numbers 1–4 and one card of the number 5. Use dot pattern cards for younger players, digit cards with more experienced players.

Rules:

Each player puts three cards, face up, on the empty boxes on the board. The rest of the pack is put face down in the middle of the table. On your turn try to 'make 5' out of two of your three cards. If two cards do add up to 5, put them on the Make 5 box. Then fill up the spaces on your board so that there are three cards face up, ready for your next turn. If you can't make 5, pick up a card from the top of the pile and pair it with one of your three cards, or put it back at the bottom of the pile if you can't use it. When the cards are used up, count the cards on each player's Make 5 box to find the winner.

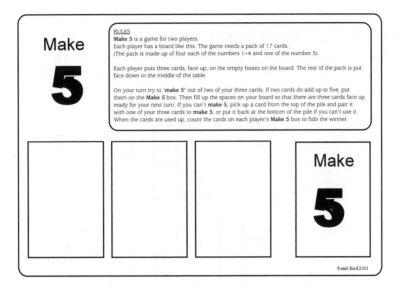

Make 5

RULES
Make 5 is a game for two players.
Each player has a board like this. The game needs a pack of 17 cards.
(The pack is made up of four each of the numbers 1–4 and one of the number 5).

Each player puts three cards, face up, on the empty boxes on the board. The rest of the pack is put face down in the middle of the table.

On your turn try to 'make 5' out of two of your three cards. If two cards do add up to five, put them on the **Make 5** box. Then fill up the spaces on your board so that there are three cards face up ready for your next turn. If you can't **make 5**, pick up a card from the top of the pile and pair it with one of your three cards to **make 5**, or put it back at the bottom of the pile if you can't use it. When the cards are used up, count the cards on each player's **Make 5** box to fidn the winner.

Make 5

Ronit Bird 2001

Tips:

Allow pupils to use their fingers, or counters, or a bead string of five large beads (all of the same colour) until they realise there are only two ways of making 5. If they don't realise on their own after playing the game more than once, tell them and then challenge them to play the game without fingers or other counting aids. The single card for 5 is introduced into the pack because otherwise the game would too often end in a draw. Alternatively, use a pack made of the numbers 1–4 but with an odd number of cards.

 Activities

Become familiar with Cuisenaire rods

Cuisenaire rods provide an excellent concrete continuous resource for exploring the numbers up to 10. Their great advantage is that their physical size can be seen, or found – by measuring against other rods – without counting. They are deliberately designed to be identified by length, with the individual colours contributing to easy recognition. Do not be tempted to label them with numbers or to divide their lengths visibly into 'ones'.

Pupils must be given time to become familiar with the rods and their colours and relative sizes before using them as mathematical models. Many useful activities can be found in Professor Sharma's *Cuisenaire Rods and Mathematics Teaching* (1993).

Some of my favourite activities are summarised here. See also my leaflet, *Some things you can do with your Cuisenaire Rods* (2002), which can be found on the CD. Encourage a lot of talk during all these activities.

1. Build a staircase, flat on the table or in the lid of the rods' box. Practise building it quickly, some-times starting with the longest rod (orange) and sometimes with the shortest rod (white).

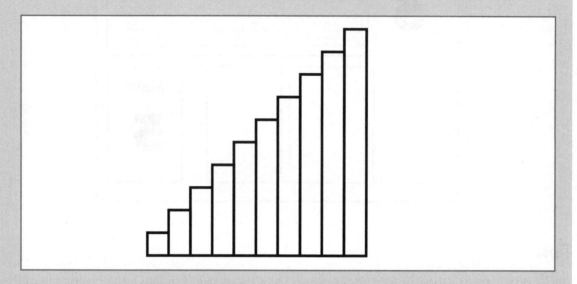

2. Match the numbers to the colours. Learn to recite the colours: white, red, light green, purple (or pink), yellow, dark green, black, brown, blue, orange. Pick out a rod at random and say its number, first with the help of the staircase and later with the staircase hidden. Say the colour and the number of the rod that is one bigger, or one smaller, than a rod picked at random.

3. Make flat patterns. Later, record the patterns with coloured pencils on 1 cm squared paper. Challenge pupils to recreate patterns that you or other pupils have made or have recorded on paper.

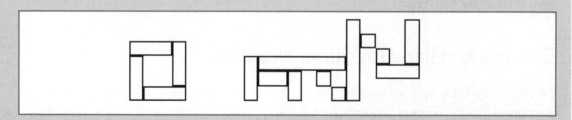

4. Make sequences. Challenge pupils to say which rod comes next in the sequence. Take one rod from a sequence while a pupil is not looking and close the gap. You can do this also for the staircase sequence. Challenge the pupil to name the missing rod and show its position in the sequence.

5. Explore relative sizes. Pick up a rod at random and ask the child to find a rod that is larger. Encourage pupils to notice that there is (usually) more than one right answer to this question. Next, ask for the rod that is only just, or one step, larger. This time there is only one right answer. Sometimes ask for a rod that is smaller than a chosen rod, or for a rod that is smaller by one.

6. Find one rod that is equal in length to two others, and vice versa. Put any two rods end to end and have the pupil first guess or estimate, and then measure, which single rod is equal in length. Next, put any two rods side by side, sometimes aligned at the left and sometimes at the right, and have the pupil estimate, then measure, which rod exactly fills the gap.

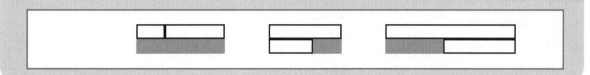

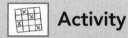 **Activity**

Explore odd and even with Cuisenaire rods and with money

Give pupils the task of measuring every rod against white rods (ones) and discussing what they find. They will, of course, find that every length of rod can be measured in ones, and that the number of units each rod is worth, is also its position in the counting sequence.

Next, have pupils experiment to find which rods can be measured exactly using red rods (twos) only.

Provide heaps of 1p and 2p coins. Have pupils make different amounts, up to 10p, in different ways, as in the example above. Next, challenge pupils to make as many of these amounts as is possible using 2p coins only.

Get children to articulate what they now understand about the words 'odd' and 'even'.

By focusing on the fact that 10 is – and always will be – even, you can extend this activity by using the rods and the coins to explain how to determine which larger numbers are odd and which are even.

Game

Odd and Even Collectors

A game for two players.

Teaching points:

◆ The game teaches children to recognise odd and even numbers up to 10.

◆ It teaches that a fair die is as likely to produce an even throw as an odd throw.

◆ At the scoring stage, it gives practice in exchanging and counting up small numbers.

Equipment needed:

◆ Cuisenaire rods.

◆ A 1–10 die or spinner.

Rules:

At the start of the game, determine which player will collect the even numbers, and which the odd numbers. The player collecting the odd numbers starts by getting an orange 10-rod (to compensate for the fact that the even numbers on a die are worth more than the odd numbers). Players then take turns to throw the die and to pick up a Cuisenaire rod to match the throw. The rod is then either kept by that player or awarded to the opponent, depending on who is collecting the odd/even numbers. After 3 rounds (a total of 6 throws) players find who is the winner by exchanging their smaller rods for orange rods wherever possible, and then counting up the total amount in their collections.

Tips:

The exchange at the end of the game is harder for the player collecting 'odd' numbers, so make sure this is not always the same person. Confusion can often result at the exchange and counting-up stage. Until pupils have had plenty of practice, it is therefore best if the teacher takes the role of banker and supervises each exchange, amidst lots of talk about what is happening.

Variation 1:

Use money instead of rods, allowing the children to collect 1p and 2p coins, and to exchange them for 10p coins at the counting-up stage. The odd collector should get a 10p coin to start the game. Real money, rather than plastic or cardboard, makes the game more exciting.

Variation 2:

A player is allowed to keep the rods or coins only if the collector of odd numbers throws an odd number on his/her turn, or the collector of even numbers throws an even number on his/her turn. In this variation the odd collector gets an extra turn, instead of being given the 10 rod or a 10p coin at the start, by being both first and last to throw the die. A game in this variation consists of 7 throws.

Game

Draw Your Race on a Number Line

A game for two or more players.

Teaching points:

◆ The game teaches children the relationship between a number track (where each number is represented by a physical area and where progress is made by counting whole numbers) and the more abstract number line (where each number is represented by a position on a line and where progress is made by counting the steps between whole numbers).

◆ The game teaches how to use an empty number line, and to understand what a number line represents.

◆ It gives practice in adding small quantities: +1, +2 and +3.

Equipment needed:

◆ A paper copy of the board for each player (see CD).

◆ A pencil and a token for each player.

◆ A 1–3 die (cover the three larger numbers with stickers).

Rules:

Take turns to throw the die and move your token along the track. Then draw the whole jump on your number line. Write how big the jump is (above the jump) and what number you have reached (under the line). If you land on the round number 10, have another turn. The winner is the first player to reach (or pass) 15.

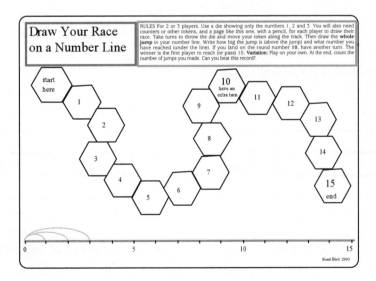

Tips:

Use this game to teach the conventions of number lines: that the movements along the line are shown as jumps drawn above the line and are labelled with the size of the jump, while the position on the number line is shown by a small perpendicular mark on the line together with a number below the line. A very useful activity at the end of the game is for each child to recreate their moves by looking at their drawn jumps. For example: First I threw a two and landed on 2, then I threw a one and got to 3, ….

Variation

This can be played as a solitaire game, aiming for the fewest throws of the die.

 Activities

Use Cuisenaire rods to learn all components of the numbers 1–10

1. Start with the key facts of a number, which are the double or near-double components. Pupils should already be familiar with these from their earlier work with dot patterns. For example, the key components of 8 are 4 and 4; the key components of 9 are 4 and 5 (or 5 and 4). Remind pupils that they know these facts and challenge them to use the rods to demonstrate that the facts are true.

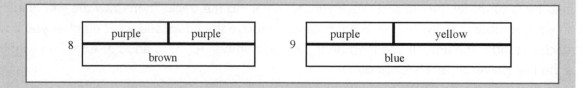

2. Take two rods of the same colour and sandwich a smaller rod between them, aligning them sometimes at the left and sometimes at the right. Have the pupil first guess, and then measure, which single rod exactly fills the gap.

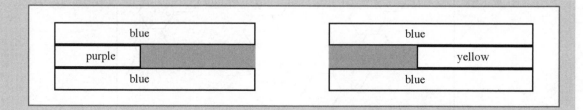

3. Explore each number in turn, finding all the components and asking lots of questions, varying the vocabulary you use. If you challenge pupils to find as many ways of making 7 as they can, you might find one pupil offering a combination such as red, red and

light green, while another offers the same combination in a different order, such a red, light green and red. This is an opportunity to discuss with pupils whether these solutions are the same, and to explore with them how combinations that are not identical may still have equal values.

4. Have pupils set out, in a logical sequence, all the ways of making a number out of two components, for example the 'story of seven' shown below, and talk about how the pattern shifts from row to row. Point out explicitly how, as soon as one of the components gets bigger by one, the other component must become one smaller to compensate, and vice versa.

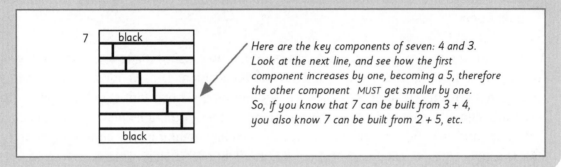

Here are the key components of seven: 4 and 3. Look at the next line, and see how the first component increases by one, becoming a 5, therefore the other component MUST get smaller by one. So, if you know that 7 can be built from 3 + 4, you also know 7 can be built from 2 + 5, etc.

 Activities

Make and read equations with Cuisenaire rods

This is one of the activities suggested by Professor Sharma in his 1993 booklet, *Cuisenaire Rods and Mathematics Teaching*.

Put any two rods end to end and have the pupil find a single rod that is the same length. Tell pupils that they have just made an equation. Children love to hear that they have made something so complex. This equation can now be read in different ways, both as additions and as subtractions. Model the different ways, pointing to the relevant rod as you say each number, before asking the pupil to do the same. For example:

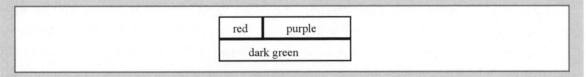

Two and four is six. (Alternate the words 'add', or 'plus' or 'and . . . more' instead of always using the word 'and'.)

Four and two is six. (Alternate the use of 'is', with 'is the same as', 'equals' or 'makes'.)

Six is equal to two and four.

Six is equal to four add two.

Six minus two is four. (Alternate the use of 'minus' with 'take away' or 'subtract'.)

Six minus four is two.

Activities

Draw and record equations in writing

1. Get the pupils to record the equations they have made in the activity above by drawing on 1 cm squared paper with coloured pencils that match the rod colours.

2. At later sessions, the original equations can be recreated by putting the rods on top of the coloured drawings. The equations can now be read in the same way as they were in the activity above. The equations can also be read, in the same variety of ways, from the pictures alone.

3. Record the equations in the more conventional way, using digits and symbols. Make sure that equations are recorded both as additions and as subtractions, in any order, so as to reinforce the relationship between addition and subtraction. Don't always put the equals sign at the end of the number sentence, otherwise pupils believe that the equal sign means 'now find the answer' instead of actually meaning 'everything on the left of this sign is equal in value to everything on the right of this sign'. That is,

not only:	$2 + 4 = 6$	$6 - 2 = 4$	$4 + 2 = 6$	$6 - 4 = 2$
but also:	$6 = 2 + 4$	$2 = 6 - 4$	$6 = 4 + 2$	$4 = 6 - 2$

4. Get pupils to turn the equations above into written number problems for other pupils to solve. That means leaving a gap in place of one of the three numbers in the equation. Show pupils how the gap can be left in any position, so long as two numbers are given from which the third can be found.

    For example, the first equation above, $2 + 4 = 6$, can be turned into written questions in three different ways: $2 + 4 = \boxed{}$, $2 + \boxed{} = 6$, or $\boxed{} + 4 = 6$. The last two show the missing-addend notation and should be read as *Two and what makes six?* and *What and four makes six?* Missing-addend work is much more difficult than a straightforward sum, because pupils must simultaneously hold two ideas in their head: the concept of addition and the concept of equality. The activity described here helps to minimise that difficulty. Note that each of the eight equations above can be rendered as three written questions.

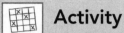 **Activity**

Make up word problems to match a given number fact

Children understand arithmetic questions much more readily when a problem is situated in a context that has some meaning for them. It is much better to ask about 'two more toys' than about the abstract '+ 2'. Similarly, although a teacher sees immediately that 'two million pounds and three million pounds' is essentially the same problem as 'two balloons and three balloons', children who do not really know what a million is will not be able to solve the first problem even when they can easily solve the second.

Pupils who have only been given word problems in order to test their understanding of abstract calculation procedures they have just been taught, will often panic when faced with mixed word problems. Their typical strategy is to pick out all the numbers, ignore the words, and guess what operation to perform on those numbers. To counter this kind of response, Sharma advocates getting children to make up problems themselves for a given number fact. He also persuades the children to insert some irrelevant number details into the problem, e.g. the age of a child, or a date, so that pupils learn to be more discerning about whether all the numbers provided are needed for a solution.

This is a good activity to do with a group, because the variety of answers will provide lots of opportunity for useful discussion. Some children may need a scribe for this exercise.

Game

Cover the Numbers, or Shut the Box

A game for one, two or more players.

Teaching points:

◆ The game teaches splitting all the numbers up to 12, in many different ways.

◆ It gives practice in adding and recombining small numbers to make the numbers up to 12.

Equipment needed:

◆ Either a manufactured version of this game (several are widely available) or my paper version (see CD) 💿 called Cover the Number, and pencils.

◆ Two 1–6 dice.

Rules:

Each player controls one set of the numbers 1–9. A player throws two dice and works out the total. The player chooses numbers from his/her set that add up to the same total, and removes them from play. The same player continues like this until no more numbers can be removed from play. The score is noted as the number of numbers left uncovered. Play now passes to the next player. The winner has the lowest score after 3 rounds.

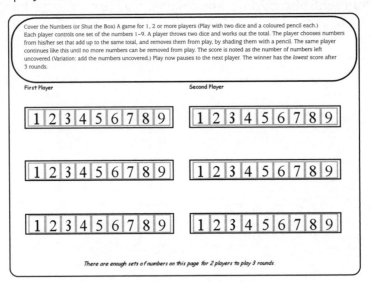

Variation 1:

This can be played as a solitaire game, with the player aiming to use all the numbers in the set.

Variation 2:

For older pupils, the score at the end of the round is calculated by adding the numbers still uncovered, with the total counting against the player. This calls for a different strategy during the game, i.e. making use of the larger numbers as components wherever possible.

Game

Clear the Deck

A solitaire game for one player.

Teaching points:

◆ The game reinforces all the number bonds of the target number. The target can be any number between 6 and 10, inclusive.

Equipment needed:

◆ A pack of cards with four cards of each digit, doctored according to the target number.

Rules:

Decide on the target and discard from the pack any digits that are equal to or greater than the target number. Shuffle the pack well. Lay out an array of cards face up, so that the number of cards on show is one less than the target number. For example, if the target is 6, keep only the numbers 1–5 in the pack and lay out five cards face up; if the target is 10, construct the pack out of the numbers 1–9 and lay out nine cards face up. Play by clearing away any two cards that add up to the target number and immediately filling the two spaces with new cards. The aim is to clear the whole pack of cards.

Tip:

Encourage the player to talk aloud as s/he clears the pairs away, e.g. *2 and 4 are 6, 1 plus 5 is 6*, etc.

Card array if the target number is 6

Array if the target number is 10

Activity

Make a bead string, in two colours, of 10 beads

You will need to find beads of the size, colour and shape to suit the age and sex of your pupils. Younger children need large unbreakable beads. Fancy shapes, such as stars, are fine as long as they are chunky enough to be easily distinguished, while fiddly shapes like clowns or crescents, should be avoided. Pupils who feel they are too old for brightly coloured plastic beads enjoy using strings made of slim wooden ovals in natural colours.

It is important to use beads of the same size, in only two colours, arranged in two groups of five. The two colours should not be too close in tone. The idea of the bead strings is that children can learn to 'see' most of the numbers up to 10 without counting in ones.

When the bead string is completed, you should be able to slide beads along it and have them stay in place. Therefore, depending on the size of the holes, some beads can be threaded on a thick cord like a shoelace, while others may need double-threading with the kind of strong nylon yarn sold for threading necklaces. Follow the instructions in the diagram below.

Children can be given a bead string as a personal calculator for the numbers up to 10, for example when learning to play a game such as 'Ten in a Bed' (see below). At first children will need to physically move the beads for any calculation; after a while it should be enough just to look at the bead string. Finally, children should be encouraged to visualise the string and do the calculation mentally.

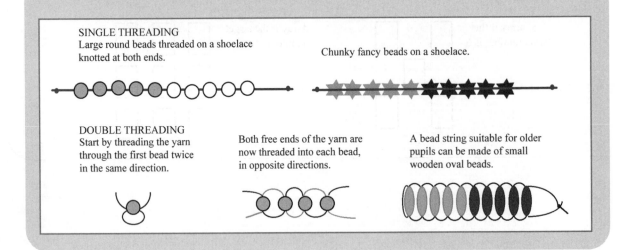

SINGLE THREADING
Large round beads threaded on a shoelace knotted at both ends.

Chunky fancy beads on a shoelace.

DOUBLE THREADING
Start by threading the yarn through the first bead twice in the same direction.

Both free ends of the yarn are now threaded into each bead, in opposite directions.

A bead string suitable for older pupils can be made of small wooden oval beads.

Activity

Learn complements of 10 with the bead string

The word 'complement' comes from the word 'complete'. The *complements of 10* or *complements to 10* are the pairs of numbers that add up to 10. These five number bonds are key facts that pupils must learn by heart. The following activities and games help teach these key facts.

1. Give children practice in 'subitising', i.e. seeing a quantity without counting. Most people can subitise very small numbers, such as 2 or 3, easily. Show a small number of beads on the string, keeping the rest hidden in your hand, and pass the other hand repeatedly back and forth in front of the beads, so that they cannot be counted. Practise first with numbers up to 3, then include 4.

2. Explain to children how they can also 'see' the numbers 6, 7 and 8, and maybe 9, because they can see numbers up to 4 and because they know that there is a colour change at five. Give lots of practice.

3. Slide the beads apart so that they form two groups. Ask children to match your pattern on their own bead strings as quickly as they can. It is obviously quicker to do this if they don't count either group first.

4. Show on the bead string how 10 can be built, or split, by sliding one bead at a time from left to right. Have the pupils copy you 'reading' the complements aloud: 1 and 9, 2 and 8, ...

Game

How Many Beads? How Many Are Hidden?

A game for two players.

Teaching points:

◆ The game gives practice in subitising small numbers.

◆ It teaches bridging though 5 (building the larger numbers, mentally, from '5 and some more').

◆ It teaches the complements to 10.

Equipment needed:

◆ A bead string for each child.

Rules:

While one child looks away, the other hides some of the beads from one end of the string in their hand, leaving the rest dangling and visible. The first child now looks and must say how many beads are showing and how many are hidden, without counting.

Activity

Find complements of 10 with Cuisenaire rods

Have the pupils build a staircase, from 10 down to 1, with Cuisenaire rods. Now get them to transform the staircase into a wall, by adding 'the complement' to the top of each rod, i.e. making each column add up to 10. It can be a moment of revelation for some children, when they discover that in the process of following these instructions they are actually building another staircase, upside down.

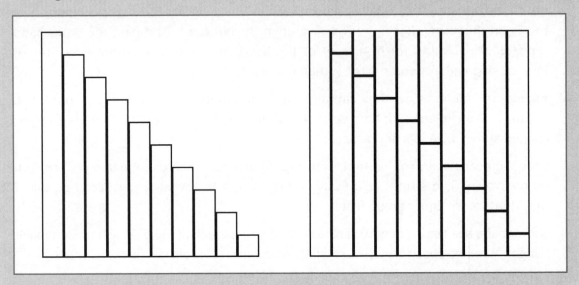

Use the wall to talk about complements to 10, to read equations, to pose addition and subtraction questions, and to write number problems, including missing-number problems, just as you did for the component work detailed earlier in this section. The only difference here is that the paired components of 10 are so important for the pupils to know that these five or six facts need more attention, and more time spent on exploring and learning them, than other number bonds.

The five (or six) complement facts are: (0 + 10)

$$1 + 9$$
$$2 + 8$$
$$3 + 7$$
$$4 + 6$$
$$5 + 5$$

Game

Complements Number Search

This is a solitaire activity, or can be turned into a competitive game by seeing which member of the group can find the most complement pairs in a limited time period.

Number searches, with a single digit written in each of the squares formed by an 8 × 8 or 10 × 10 grid, are very easy to make. They are just as easy, and instructive, for pupils to make for each other. Players must circle any neighbouring or diagonally adjacent pairs of numbers that are complements to 10. A digit may contribute to more than one pair of complements.

Search for   **complements to 10**

Find two numbers next to each other that add up to 10. Circle them.

1	8	2	0	5	4	6	9
9	3	6	4	5	5	3	2
7	5	1	9	3	2	8	8
1	3	7	1	7	1	5	1
9	5	4	4	6	9	0	8
1	5	0	8	2	9	1	9
6	3	5	5	2	4	5	5
5	7	4	2	8	6	0	6

Game

Complements Ping-Pong

A game for a group of pupils.

Teaching points:

◆ The game gives practice in fast recall of the five complement facts.

Equipment needed:

◆ None, although it would be useful to have a way of generating random numbers from 0 to 10, e.g. a die or a pack of number cards.

Rules:

The teacher calls out a number from 0 to 10 and each pupil must immediately 'bounce back' its complement to 10. If the pupil is too slow, s/he is deemed to have dropped the ball and is out, until the next round.

Tip:

This is a quick game that makes a good warm-up activity for the start of a lesson.

Game

Ten in a Bed

'Ten in a Bed' was once a commercially produced game that is, sadly, no longer available. What I show on the CD, therefore, are the rules, which can be photocopied on A5 paper or card to become the reverse of a game board. The pupils should draw a bed, with people or animals lying in bed, on the other side of their own game board.

This is a game for two or three players.

Teaching points:

◆ The game reinforces the complements of 10 facts.

Equipment needed:

◆ An A5 board for each player (see CD).

◆ A pack of 36 dot cards (for younger players) or digit cards, the packs being made of four cards of each of the digits 1–9.

Rules:

Each player gets four cards to start. Players take turns to pick up a card from the remainder pile until all the cards in the pile are gone. As soon as a player has two cards that add up to 10, the player puts the pair of cards to bed (collecting them on the bed picture on the board) and then takes another card from the pile, which may help to make a new pair that can be put to bed. The winner is the player with most cards put to bed.

Tips:

Add an extra card showing the number 10 to the pack, or use a pack with an odd number of cards, to prevent the game ending too often in a draw. Tell the pupils they are not allowed to count while playing this game, but that they may use a bead string as a personal calculator, until they know the complements to 10 by heart.

Variation:

Players are allowed three (or more) cards that add up to 10, instead of just pairs of cards.

LIB

Activities

Explore and learn the doubles up to 5 + 5

1. Use nuggets or bricks, and use a mirror to see what happens when the pattern is doubled. Then have the pupils make the doubled pattern without a mirror. Pupils should practise reading the double patterns in several ways, e.g. *Double 2 is 4*, or *When 2 is doubled you get 4*, or *2 and another 2 makes 4*, or *Twice 2 is 4*, or *2 times 2 is 4*. If the pupils only use the formulation *2 and 2 is 4*, they will get into the habit of thinking that doubling is all about adding, whereas it is really about multiplication.

> *Hold a mirror perpendicular to the desk top, to illuminate the meaning of 'double'.*

2. Have children make the dot patterns for the numbers 1–10 out of nuggets or other discrete concrete materials and remind them that they are built from doubles or near-doubles patterns. Pupils must say what half of each of the even numbers is, and be able to explain in their own words what the problem is with finding half of the odd numbers.

3. Give pupils one of each of the five smallest rods out of the Cuisenaire box. They must take a second rod of each colour, lay it end to end next to its matching pair, and then find the single rod that measures the same. Pupils should now read the equation they have made: as well as all the different ways they have already learned from earlier activities, they can now practise using the words *twice, double, times 2, 2 times, half, halve, half of, divided by 2, split equally into two parts, divided into two equal parts*, etc., as they read the equations. They can also record the equations on paper as additions and subtractions, as in earlier activities, and now also as multiplications (×2) and divisions (÷2).

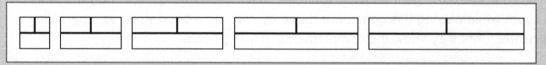

4. On 1 cm squared paper, fold along a straight line and draw over the fold. Have children colour in squares, or stick small round stickers in squares, so that all the even numbers in turn are shown with half of the amount on either side of the fold line. The fold line can sometimes be horizontal, at other times vertical on the page. Pupils should read these representations both as double and half facts, and can also record the double and half facts using words and all four operations signs. See the illustration below.

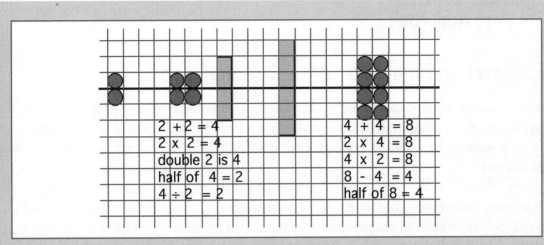

5. Depending on the age and conceptual understanding of the pupils, this may be a good opportunity to discuss what happens when halving odd numbers. Pupils can cut out the relevant number of squares from paper with large squares and fold it in half it to show that half of, say, 7 is $3\frac{1}{2}$.

Activities

Estimate and measure using Cuisenaire rods

Many mathematical educationalists recommend estimating exercises as a way of building number sense. Indeed, consistently giving wildly inaccurate estimates of small numbers can, like the inability to count backwards, be a quick way to identify children who may have dyscalculia.

Estimating can be achieved in the brain by assessing quantity or by assessing spatial coverage, or a combination of both. Therefore it is very important to vary the size and shape of your single unit when pupils are engaged in estimating activities.

Here are some activities using Cuisenaire rods. The advantage of using them is that the pupils can check their estimates by measuring instead of counting.

1. Out of a pile of no more than 20 white rods, or other 1 cm cubes, take a small handful and drop the cubes onto the lid of a Cuisenaire rods box, letting the cubes remain in the random pattern in which they fall. Pass your hand, or a sheet of paper, back and forth over the cubes, so that the pupil is forced to estimate, or guess, the quantity without counting. After making a guess, children can shake the cubes into a straight line against a side of the box lid and should then use the larger Cuisenaire rods to measure the length of the row of cubes and thus check the accuracy of their guess.

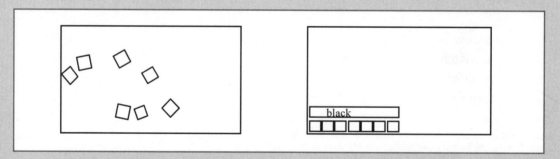

2. Pupils throw a 1–3 die and take one rod to match each throw. They collect the rods by putting them in a row, end-to-end, on top of an orange 10-rod, or on a row of 10 squares outlined on 1 cm squared paper. In this way pupils can see how the smaller amounts build up to 10. After every turn, the pupil must say how many s/he has so far, not by counting, but by guessing and then measuring against a single coloured rod. Pupils can race against each other to be the one to cover their 10 in the fewest throws. Conduct this activity with the rods sometimes set out horizontally and sometimes vertically.

3. Identify objects for the pupils to measure, e.g. a book or a chair. Pupils must first guess, and then measure, how many whole orange rods they can fit along the length or the height of each object. As only the 10-unit rods are being used, you can choose objects that are up to 10 rods in length or height, i.e. up to a metre.

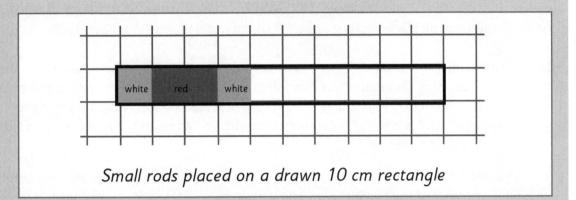

Small rods placed on a drawn 10 cm rectangle

4. Provide pupils with a page full of drawn straight lines, each measuring a whole number of centimetres less than or equal to 10 cm and drawn at various angles to each other, i.e. not all horizontal or vertical on the page. Pupils must estimate the length of each line. Pupils check their estimates by measuring the line against a single Cuisenaire rod.

   Pupils can prepare this activity for each other. Drawing straight lines accurately to whole centimetres is a skill that needs practice. Dyspraxic pupils should be given a ruler with a handle.

5. Pupils throw a die and, starting from a line drawn on the floor, take as many steps forward as matches the throw. Depending on the length of their stride, different pupils will cover a different amount of ground for the same throw of the die. Pupils mark where they have reached and estimate or guess how far they have moved. Pupils then use a metre rule to verify their estimate. If possible (as we are still working with numbers up to 10 at this stage) have them use one of those metre sticks with a channel running along the centre, into which Cuisenaire rods or Dienes longs can be fitted, so that they are thinking in 10 cm lengths as the units of measurement that build up to 1 metre.

Activities

Focus on plus/minus 1 and plus/minus 2

Remind pupils that adding and subtracting the small quantities 1 and 2 have already formed part of their earlier work, for example the Cuisenaire rods activities on making and reading equations and also their investigations into the components of all the numbers up to 10.

1. Be explicit about the fact that when 1 is added the result is the next number in the counting sequence, and that when 1 is subtracted the result is the previous number in the counting sequence. Plus 2 and minus 2 are achieved by following the same procedure twice, i.e. +2 is not the next number but the one after, and -2 is not the previous number but the one before.

2. Take a small number of counters or nuggets. The pupil can arrange them into the familiar dot patterns, or may count them into a straight line. Use a piece of card to screen the counters. Slide one (and later, two) counters from under the screen, showing the pupil how many have been extracted. The pupil must say how many are left under the screen, without using fingers or other aids. Repeat the exercise by displaying and then adding one, or two, items to a group that were seen but are now hidden under a screen.

   A slightly harder activity is to screen a small number of counted items, as before, but now ask pupils to tell you how many must be taken out so as to leave only one (and later, two) under the screen. It is this kind of activity that helps pupils realise that a problem such as 8 – 7 can be solved by the plus/minus 1 strategy, even though the number 1 does not appear in the question.

3. Give pupils a paper number track, which is built out of 10 large squares or rectangles. At first, allow pupils to write the numbers in digits in the spaces on the track; at a later stage do the same activity on empty, unlabelled, tracks that have a visible division separating the two groups of five. Call out a number and instructions for adding or subtracting 1 or 2 to the number, instructions which pupils follow by putting a token on the track as quickly as possible. Use as varied a vocabulary as you can manage when calling out instructions. For example, for the number 5 and the instruction +1: *One more than 5, The number that is 5 and 1 more, The amount that is 1 greater than 5, The sum of 5 and 1, The sum total of 1 and 5, The total of 5 and 1, One plus 5, One add 5, One added to 5, Five and 1 together, Five increased by 1, An increase of 1 from 5.*

4. Pupils pick a Cuisenaire rod at random and are instructed first to show the rod for that number plus 1, and then the rod for that number minus 1 (or vice versa). Pupils should notice that this activity results in them showing adjacent rods from the rods staircase, a sequence with which they are already familiar.

5. Have pupils make and read equations involving plus or minus 1 or 2 with Cuisenaire rods, which they then record on paper. Encourage pupils to turn the rods upside down or back to front every so often, to help them understand that the equation is produced by the relationship between the numbers, not the order in which the numbers are presented. Pay special attention to those equations where 1, or 2, is the answer to a subtraction problem, e.g. not only 7 – 2 = 5, but also 7 – 5 = 2 and 2 = 7 – 5.

Game

Who Has the Most Equations?

This game is for two or three players.

Teaching points:

◆ The game gives practice in adding and subtracting 1 or 2.

◆ It teaches pupils to recognise on which occasions they can use the plus/minus 1 or 2 strategies.

◆ It shows that the plus/minus 1 or 2 strategies can be used even when the numbers 1 or 2 do not appear on the left of the equal sign.

◆ It gives practice in making and writing simple equations.

Equipment needed:

◆ Two 1–6 dice.

◆ Paper and pencil for each player.

Rules:

Players take turns to throw both dice and to write down any number problems for which they can use the plus/minus 1 or 2 strategies. They must complete the equation with the correct answer.

For example, if they were to throw two 2s, they could write two equations, each of which would earn them a point: 2 + 2 = 4 and 2 – 2 = 0. If they were to throw a 4 and a 3, they could write three equations: 4 – 3 = 1, 4 – 1 = 3 and 3 + 1 = 4 (or 1 + 3 = 4), which could earn them three points in total. However, if they were to throw two 5s, there are no possible equations for which these strategies could be used. The winner, at the end of a certain number of turns, or a certain length of time, is the one with the most correct equations.

Tip:

Tell pupils that they will get points for each equation, and remind them to look out for both additions and subtractions, but let them find out for themselves when they can win more than one or two points. (Of the 36 possible combinations of two dice, only 21 produce different combinations, and of these only 5 combinations will produce a situation where no points can be scored.)

Variation:

Play with one 6-sided and one 10-sided die, which will extend the possible combinations, but will also produce a few more situations where no points can be scored.

Activity

Compare the difference and equalise

This activity is presented at three levels of difficulty, all on the same activity sheet (see CD), and is designed to teach pupils to think about subtraction as something other than 'taking away'.

Pupils use dice to generate two numbers to compare. They record the numbers as a subtraction number sentence and practise interpreting it as a subtraction, a difference problem and an equalising problem, before finding and recording the solution.

The equipment needed will depending on which level of difficulty a pupil is working at: pupils working at the most basic level should be given counters or other small objects; pupils working at a higher level need Cuisenaire rods. All pupils need two 6-sided dice, one showing 0–5 and the other showing 5–10, and a pencil.

Teaching points:

- The activity gives practice in subtraction, which most pupils find harder than addition.

- It teaches that finding the difference can be expressed as subtraction, or as a missing-addend problem.

- It teaches that equalising two amounts can also be expressed as subtraction, or as a missing-addend sum.

- It reinforces the relationship between addition and subtraction.

- It lays the groundwork for understanding complementary addition, which is the most useful subtraction strategy to teach any pupil who has difficulty with arithmetic.

Tips:

The activity sheet, which can be found on the CD should, at first, be folded before photocopying, so as to present each pupil with only the appropriate level of difficulty. Later, pupils can be given the whole sheet to decide for themselves at which level to work.

Activities

Hidden quantity subtraction

1. Take a small handful of small objects, such as buttons, bricks or pencils. Ask a pupil to count the objects into a bag, which can be transparent. While pupils look away, take some items out of the bag, keep them hidden but allow pupils to examine what remains in the bag. Pupils now record what just happened, on paper, as a missing-number subtraction problem, e.g. 9 – ☐ = 3. Finally, pupils must solve the problem and find what quantity was 'subtracted' or 'taken away'. Pupils could get into pairs to do this activity with each other.

2. Put a secret quantity of objects into a bag while pupils look away. The bag must not be transparent. Pupils look back, and while they are looking, take some of the objects out of the bag and display them, at the same time opening the bag to show how many items remain. Pupils must record this operation as a missing-quantity subtraction problem, e.g. ☐ – 6 = 3, before solving it.

Pupils may find these activities quite challenging, even when the numbers are kept below 10. A similar activity is recommended earlier for adding and subtracting 1 or 2. These activities should be practised until pupils can solve missing-number subtraction problems for numbers below 10, without the props.

Activity

Teach complementary addition

Step 1

Take a small number of nuggets or counters, and ask the pupil to count them while moving them into a straight line. Decide on a small number to subtract from this quantity, and ask the pupil to remove this quantity from the start of the line, then from the end of the line, then from the body of the row. Each time the pupil should count how many counters remain. Be explicit that it makes no difference to the solution whether an amount is subtracted from the beginning, or from the end of a quantity (or, indeed, from the middle). Have pupils repeat this exercise as many times as is necessary to convince themselves that this is always true.

Step 2

Explain to the pupil that step 1 has involved 'mechanical arithmetic', i.e. objects have been physically moved around after which an answer has been found by counting. Mechanical arithmetic does not help us to learn to perform mental arithmetic. Mental arithmetic involves keeping track in your mind as you work through the steps of a calculation until you reach the solution.

Step 3

Now set out a row of nine nuggets from left to right in a row, and tell the pupil you need to subtract six, and that you want to try to keep track of where you are in the calculation as you work through it, so as to learn the best way to solve this problem mentally.

Step 4

In your attempt now to take six away from the end of the row – the right-hand side – you will be involved in a complex double-counting procedure where you are counting up (1, 2, 3, 4, 5, 6) the amount that you need to subtract, while counting down (9, 8, 7, 6, 5, 4, 3) the amount that remains at each step. Make this performance as hard and as complicated as possible. As you subtract each nugget, move it slightly away from the rest in the row. Because the two counts are simultaneous, you will be saying something like: *I take one away, that leaves eight, now I'm subtracting two which leaves seven, ...*

Step 5

Show how much easier it is to take away the six from the start of the row – the left-hand side. Now there are two single counts, not simultaneous counts, and both are going up in the same direction. Start from the left, moving each nugget away slightly as you touch it and count up 1, 2, 3, 4, 5, 6. Pause and say that these are the six you are taking away. Now continue counting up to find the answer: 1, 2, 3.

Step 6

Ask the pupil to explain back to you, with the nine nuggets, what you have just shown in the last two steps. Now hide the nuggets, and ask the pupil to work through the solution aloud, using only the second method, i.e. using complementary addition.

 Activity

Complementary addition on a number line

Show how complementary addition can be modelled on an empty number line. To do this, label the beginning of the line with zero and encourage the pupil to scribble away part of the line, to represent the quantity that is being subtracted or taken away. But insist that the amount being subtracted is to be taken from the beginning of the line, like the example below.

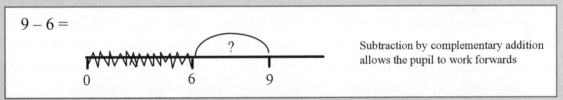

$9 - 6 =$

Subtraction by complementary addition allows the pupil to work forwards

There are two main benefits from working in this way. Firstly, pupils can always work in the forward direction. Except for very easy subtractions such as minus 1 or 2 when it would be normal to work backwards, encourage pupils to go forwards. Every pupil will find it easier to work forwards, and it is especially helpful for those with dyscalculia or other specific maths difficulties. It follows that work on a number line will always be in the forward direction, thus eliminating the need for arrows, which is a bonus for pupils with directional difficulties. Secondly, the same diagram models both $9 - 6 = \Box$ and $6 + \Box = 9$, thus reinforcing the relationship between addition and subtraction.

After practising this technique many times, pupils can skip the scribbling-out stage, if they are comfortable doing so, and simply start their labelling of the line at whatever number beyond zero they require.

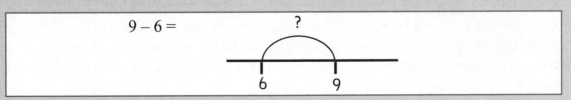

$9 - 6 =$

Activity

Use reasoning to find near-complements and near-doubles

Remind pupils of the earlier activities where they investigated the 'story' of each number with Cuisenaire rods, and when they first used a bead string. During both these activities, there should have been a lot of discussion, and some explicit teaching, about how the different facts about a particular number are related to each other. For example, during the component work the teacher should have pointed out to pupils this important observation: as soon as one component becomes one unit larger, the other component must become one unit smaller to compensate, e.g. 4 + 5 = 3 + 6. During the bead string work, pupils should have noticed that as soon as one bead is moved along the string from one group to the other, the first group is made smaller by one and the second group is automatically enlarged by one.

This kind of understanding allows pupils to derive new facts from the complement and doubles facts they already know. They learn to understand that they can adjust numbers to make a calculation easier for themselves, and to reason that any adjustment in one direction must be balanced by an adjustment in the opposite direction.

For example, if you know that 2 + 8 = 10 (which you do, because 2 and 8 are complements of 10), then you can reason that 2 + 7 = 9. Or that 3 + 8 = 11. Or that 7 + 2 = 8 + 1. Similarly, if you know that 3 + 3 = 6, you can derive the solution to the near-doubles facts: 2 + 3, 3 + 2, 3 + 4 or 4 + 3.

Put one of the known complements or doubles facts up on the board, and ask pupils to find the related near-complements and near-doubles facts that can be derived. It is more important, at this stage, to teach the pupils to recognise pairs of numbers that are almost doubles, or almost complements, than it is for them to find the actual answers to the sums.

 Activity

Identify which strategy works best in different situations

Let the pupils throw dice to generate random addition and subtraction number problems, or present pupils with a page full of problems (an example can be found on the CD). Discuss with the pupils which are the best strategies to use for each problem. Counting up or down in ones is only considered a good strategy if there are no more than two steps to be counted.

Give points for identifying a good strategy, rather than for a correct answer. Note that some problems can be solved by more than one good strategy, e.g. the answer to 5 + 4 can be found because it is a near-double fact (and so can be derived from 5 + 5 or 4 + 4) or because it is a near-complement fact (and so can be derived from 5 + 5 or from 6 + 4).

Activities

Use money for component work

Using money gives a new dimension to component work because coins come in specific denominations. These activities, therefore, give practice in splitting and recombining numbers in numerous new ways. However, remember that money is more abstract than base-10 materials: the 2 cent coin, for instance, is only worth twice the 1 cent coin because we say so, not for any logical or mathematical reason such as size or mass.

For all these activities, provide 1p, 2p, 5p and 10p coins (or 1 cent, 2 cent, 5 cent and 10 cent coins).

1. Take a small handful of 2p coins. The pupils must find the amount by counting in twos.

2. Take a few 2p coins and add to them a 5p coin. Show pupils how to start with the 5p and then count in twos starting from the odd number.

3. Teach pupils to count a collection of mixed coins by starting with the largest denominations.

4. Throw a 1–10 die. Match the throw with coins, first using the maximum number of coins (let children discover for themselves that this always means using 1p coins alone), then using the minimum number of coins.

5. Take a small handful of coins. The pupils must say how many 1p coins would be equivalent in value.

6. Take a small handful of coins that add up to an even number. How many 2p coins are equivalent in value?

7. Make small amounts of money out of different combinations of coins. How much does the pupil need to add to each collection to make 10p? (Let pupils discover for themselves that this is a complement question.)

8. Give pupils a 10p coin and send them 'shopping' for various small cheap items. For example, a pencil might cost 2p, or a rubber 3p. The pupils must work out the expected change after buying single items or combinations of items. Sometimes phrase the question as *How much money will you / do you have left to spend?* as pupils do not readily understand that this question means the same as the more common 'how much change' question.

   If one pupil buys small items while another gives change, the shopkeeper must give the change in the most efficient manner, i.e. using the smallest number of coins.

9. An extension of the shopping activity above is to ask the pupils to work out mentally how many pencils or rubbers they can afford to buy with only 10p to spend. Ask pupils to identify which prices use up the whole amount, and which result in change or money left over.

10. Give the pupils a small amount of money and challenge them to put together the same amount of money with a given number of coins. For example, give a 10p coin and ask the pupils to use five coins for the same amount, or five coins one of which is a 5p, or five coins none of which is a 5p.

11. Get pupils to make up problems modelled on the activity above for each other to solve on paper. For example:

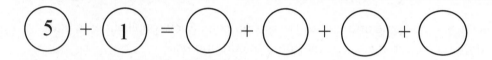

SECTION 2

Basic calculation with numbers above 10

Overview

This section continues to focus on giving pupils techniques to replace the impractical strategy of counting in ones for basic calculations. Earlier activities have already targeted the 'counting trap': the situation in which children use counting inappropriately because they know so few basic facts by heart, which in turn becomes a process that is so laborious and prone to error that new facts cannot be stored in their long-term memory. Many pupils who have difficulties cling to their old habits when they cannot see the benefits of changing them. It is only at the stage when calculations involve larger numbers that pupils begin to accept the need to learn and practise different techniques that will lead to more efficient calculation strategies.

Concrete materials, and Cuisenaire rods in particular, continue to be used in this section of the book to help children build sound cognitive models. The emphasis should always be on the understanding that needs to underpin mental calculation, and never on using the materials to find any answer mechanically. Empty number lines, which were introduced in the previous section, appear frequently in the following activities as a transition between concrete and abstract work. The emptiness of the number lines in the transition stages is important: empty number lines have been shown by research to be a powerful and flexible tool for reflecting children's own informal strategies and for supporting mental calculation. Neither the concrete stage nor the transition stage can be rushed.

Children with dyscalculia and dyslexia may have severe problems with their short-term and long-term memory. It is therefore very important to minimise the amount that pupils have to know by heart, both in terms of facts and procedures. The activities and games presented here focus on those techniques that have the widest applications, such as bridging through 10 and subtracting using complementary addition. Alongside these key ideas, the activities teach pupils how to use logic and reasoning to derive new facts from those they already know.

What are the main problems?

◆ Poor number sense, i.e. no feel for the actual size of even small quantities, no feel for the relative sizes of different numbers, poor estimating abilities, no intuitive understanding of how the number system works and how the decade structure has repeating patterns, insecurity about the concept of place value, etc.

◆ Long-term memory difficulties, including weaknesses in sequential memory, auditory memory and memory for language-encoded facts, exacerbated by problems retrieving facts from long-term memory.

◆ Short-term working memory weaknesses, resulting in pupils going off on a tangent, or giving up before a full solution is reached, because they find it too difficult to keep in mind what the problem is asking, at the same time as having to work on solving it.

◆ Confusion about whether adding or subtracting means counting the numbers, or the intervals between numbers.

◆ Not noticing patterns, relationships and connections between numbers, situations or other maths topics.

◆ Relying on cumbersome counting methods, resulting in memory overload and frequent errors.

◆ Using such inefficient calculation methods – in particular, counting in ones – that the connection between the question and the answer is lost. This means that new facts cannot be stored in long-term memory.

◆ Feeling overwhelmed when too much information is presented at once, for example a 100-square with 100 labelled numbers, or worksheets and textbooks with pages that are too busy and cluttered.

How to help

◆ Break each topic into tiny steps. Do not move on too quickly to larger numbers. Include lots of revision.

◆ Allow pupils as much thinking time as they need to complete any calculation, including oral work. Time constraints produce stress, which is the enemy of learning.

◆ Use appropriate concrete materials that will help build cognitive models. At this stage, that means continuous material such as Cuisenaire rods or Dienes blocks. Discrete materials that have to be counted in ones should be phased out by the time pupils are working with numbers above 20.

◆ Let the pupils manipulate the concrete materials themselves. Do not use them only for demonstration purposes, or only to illustrate written calculations.

◆ Recording the maths in writing should follow practical experience with concrete materials, not precede it.

◆ Allow informal jottings before teaching standard written notation.

◆ Continue to offer concrete materials until well after a pupil stops asking to use them. Remember that the transitional stage between concrete and abstract work is pictorial or diagrammatic work.

◆ Avoid visual presentations that contain too much information. For example, introduce 100-squares carefully, as an extension of the number track. When making worksheets or choosing textbooks, ensure there is plenty of white space on the page.

◆ Ask lots of open questions. Encourage the pupils to explain and talk through everything they do, in their own words.

◆ Encourage the use of empty number lines, first as diagrammatic models and later as a model for pupils to visualise and manipulate in the mind's eye.

◆ After the individual numbers up to 10 are well understood, do not assume that pupils can make the connection to all larger numbers. Spend time on the numbers between 10 and 20, spelling out as many connections to earlier learning as possible, before moving on.

◆ Teach strategies to avoid counting in ones. Be explicit with pupils that the strategies deliberately encourage seeing numbers as being built out of component chunks, not ones.

◆ Teach component work in a way that reinforces the connection between partitioning and recombining, between adding and subtracting.

◆ Teach and practise bridging through 10, once complements to 10 are known by heart.

◆ Teach subtraction as complementary addition. Tell pupils always to use complementary addition in preference to subtraction (unless there are only one or two backward steps).

◆ Minimise the number of facts that have to be known by heart.

◆ Teach explicitly how to reason from known or given facts.

◆ Don't overload pupils with too many strategies. Even if you demonstrate or explain several different strategies, allow each pupil to practise and learn only a minimum number of key strategies.

◆ Focus on the 'Basic 8' strategies and show pupils how to identify which kinds of problems can be solved by each strategy you teach.

◆ Pay attention to the vocabulary you use and be sure to vary the terms and sentence constructions.

◆ Encourage pupils to make up their own number problems and their own word problems.

 Activity

Connect the numbers 10–20 with the numbers below 10

Remind pupils of their earlier work with dot patterns (see Section 1). Use dot pattern cards to make the numbers between 11 and 20, by using one 10-spot card and one other card representing a number of units.

Ask pupils to visualise one of the dot patterns, and answer questions about the number itself (which is revision) and about the number that is 10 more (which encourages pupils to make the desired connection). Vary the vocabulary and format of the questions. For example:

Put the pattern of 9 in your mind.

What must be added to 5 to make 9?

So, what do I need to add to 15 if I need 19?

What is left if you take 5 from 19?

How much bigger is 19 than 15?

How much more is 19 than 5?

If you have 19 sweets and I only have 5, how many more do you have than I have?

How far is 9 from 10?

So, how far is 9 from 20?

How much older is 9-year-old Tom than his sister who is 4?

Sally is 19 years old. How much older is she than the 4-year-old?

 Activities

Focus on the 'teen' numbers

Point out to pupils that the names for the 'teen' numbers are inconsistent. Pupils need to be aware that in the numbers 13–19, the first digit one hears or says is the last digit one reads or writes.

1. Give lots of practice in *building* the numbers between 10 and 20 concretely from materials such as base-10 blocks, Cuisenaire rods, and coins.
   Give practice in *writing* teen numbers in digits, both by labelling amounts made from concrete materials, and from dictation.
   Provide practice in *reading* the teen numbers, presented in a random order.

2. Make the teen numbers using a spike abacus. Have pupils match these numbers with concrete materials. Pupils then record the number in digits.

3. Have pupils sketch the teen numbers, both as if they were made on a spike abacus, and as if they were made from Dienes blocks. Present the numbers to the pupils in words, in writing. Pupils complete their sketches with the number written in digits.

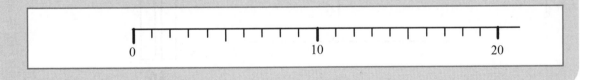

4. Let pupils practise adding 1 and subtracting 1 from all the teen numbers. Soon, extend this to adding or subtracting 2. Sometimes ask pupils to visualise the operations and answer orally, e.g. *Look at your sketch of 15 and tell me how many there would be if you had one less. What about 2 more than 15?* At other times have pupils write the additions or subtractions as number problems, e.g. 15 + 1 = 16, 2 + 15 = 17, 14 = 15 – 1.

5. Encourage pupils to make up varied word problems for the plus/minus one/two equations in the above activity.

6. Locate the teen numbers on a skeleton number line. Present pupils with a number line like the one below, on which round numbers (multiples of 10) are marked and labelled and on which there are marks but no labels for the numbers in between. Pupils must locate a teen number, chosen at random by the teacher, and write it under the line as quickly as possible. Provide a fresh skeleton number line for every two or three numbers, so that pupils are forced to locate new numbers in relation to the round numbers, rather than from previous answers.

Activities

Explore the numbers between 10 and 20 with Cuisenaire rods

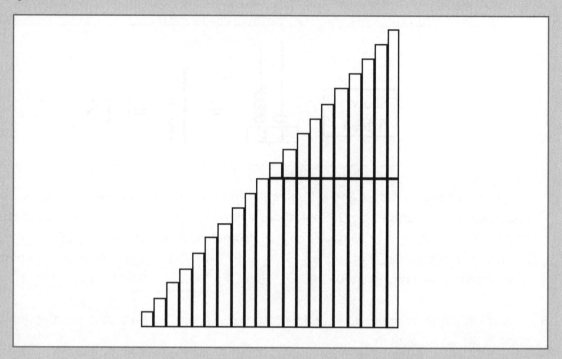

1. Have pupils build a staircase out of Cuisenaire rods. Extend the staircase to 19 (or to 20 if large boxes of rods are available). Pupils are often surprised to see the familiar 1–10 staircase repeating itself.

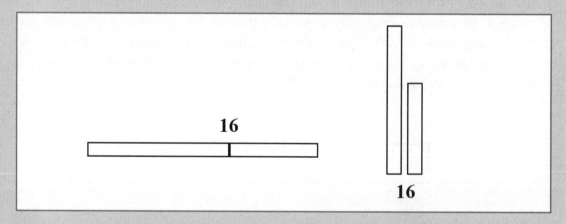

2. Pull out individual steps from the staircase for pupils to name orally and in writing. Show how these numbers can be laid out end to end, vertically (as in the staircase), horizontally, or side by side to emphasise their tens-and-units structure.

3. Ask pupils to solve simple additions by estimating the total of two rods and then measuring against other Cuisenaire rods. For example, for the question 8 + 8, pupils take out two brown rods and lay them end to end. Ask pupils to estimate whether the length of this 'train' is more or less than an orange 10-rod. More or less than two orange rods? At this stage pupils should lay one orange rod under their sum, aligned at the left, and guess, or use trial and error to measure, what other rod exactly fills the gap.

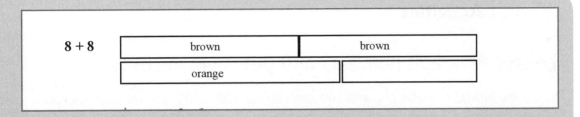

Encourage pupils to notice during this exercise that just as the orange 10-rod is two units *bigger* than one of the original components, so must the gap-filling rod be two units *smaller* than the other component. This is the kind of reasoning approach that pupils will find invaluable when they have to perform mental additions without concrete materials.

4. Pupils should 'read' the equation they make during the activity above, in just the same way as they read equations for rods that totalled less than 10, in the Section 1 activities. As they speak, the pupils should point to each rod or quantity they mention. For example:

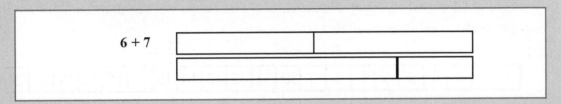

Six add seven is thirteen.

Seven and six is thirteen.

Thirteen is equal to six and seven.

Thirteen minus seven is six.

Sometimes, pupils can record the equations in writing. Challenge them to find just as many subtraction formats as addition sums. For example:

6 + 7 = 13	13 − 6 = 7
7 + 6 = 13	13 − 7 = 6
13 = 6 + 7	7 = 13 − 6
13 = 7 + 6	6 = 13 − 7

5. You can introduce flexible thinking about partitioning (more on this later) by adding a final step to the equations activity above: treat the solution to the addition as a tens-and-unit addition as well as a single two-digit number. In the 6 + 7 example, this entails reading the equation as *six add seven is equal to ten and three*, as well as all the other ways of reading it already listed above. There are two ways to record this in writing: for example, the 8 + 8 addition is recorded both as 8 + 8 = 10 + 6, and as 8 + 8 = 10 + 6 = 16 (or 16 = 10 + 6 = 8 + 8). This way of thinking encourages pupils to connect simple computation with the concept of place value.

This exercise also helps pupils understand the true meaning of the equal sign, which too many children believe to mean 'now find the answer', instead of actually meaning *everything on the left of the sign is equal in value to whatever is on the right of the sign.*

Activities

Locate two-digit numbers and put them in context

1. Locate individual numbers on a 100-bead string. 100-strings are sold commercially and usually have a colour change after every 10 beads. Call out a two-digit number. Pupils race to touch the bead that represents that number. Some counting is inevitable in this exercise but, by making it a race, pupils will have to find the most efficient counting strategies, e.g. counting first in tens and then in twos, or counting back from the next round ten for locating a number ending in 8 or 9.

2. Locate numbers on a number track made of labelled squares on paper. Start with numbers up to 30 or up to 50, before extending the activity to numbers up to 100. Note that tracks that are long enough for 50 or more numbers are cumbersome to use, a fact you should point out while doing this activity, so that pupils will see that there are advantages to using 100-squares instead.

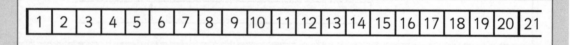

As an additional exercise, once the number is located pupils must say which are the two nearest round numbers (multiples of 10) that lie on either side of the targeted number.

3. Sometimes, ask pupils to locate numbers on tracks on which most of the numbers are blanked out, so that pupils have to find numbers in relation to others, with a minimum of counting.

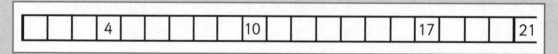

4. Locate numbers in a 100-field. Note that 100-squares are not popular with children who have maths difficulties, because there is an overwhelming amount of information on them. To introduce the 100-square gradually, while also demonstrating the logic behind it, get pupils to construct their own. Give pupils a number track like the one described in the two activities above, i.e. made of numbered squares on paper. Have pupils cut the track after every 10 numbers. Show pupils how to reassemble the strips into the top part of a 100-square (using a 1–30 track or a 1–50 track). At a later stage have pupils make a whole 100-square by cutting up a 1–100 track.

Pupils should practise locating individual numbers as quickly as they can. Ask pupils also to find and name the two round numbers between which the targeted number lies.

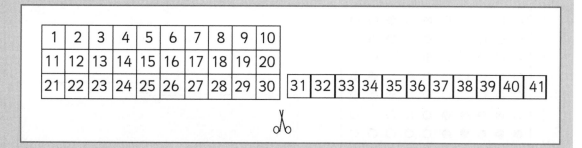

5. Make an overlay to fit the 100-square. The overlay should be opaque and should show all the squares but not their number labels. Cut out a few squares through which the numbers on the labelled 100-square can be seen. Ask pupils to locate numbers that are hidden, by reasoning in as few steps as possible – i.e. *not* counting in ones – from the numbers that they can see through the cut-outs. Rotate the overlay to produce four different positions for the cut-outs.

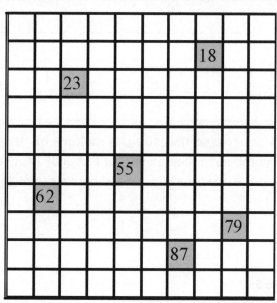

Laminated paper overlay for a 100-square. The shaded squares have been cut out so that the numbers beneath can be seen.

6. Locate numbers on a Slavonic abacus. A Slavonic abacus is an abacus made of 100 beads on ten horizontal spokes, in two colours arranged so that there is a colour change after every five beads and five rows. Locating an individual number is very similar to using the 100-square above, the difference being that there are no number labels. Despite this, counting is kept to a minimum because of the colour changes. For children already familiar with an abacus like this, you can provide a paper abacus for further practice, like the one shown below.

Lots of interesting ideas about using a Slavonic abacus, or a paper abacus, can be found in Eva Grauberg's 1998 book, *Elementary Mathematics and Language Difficulties*.

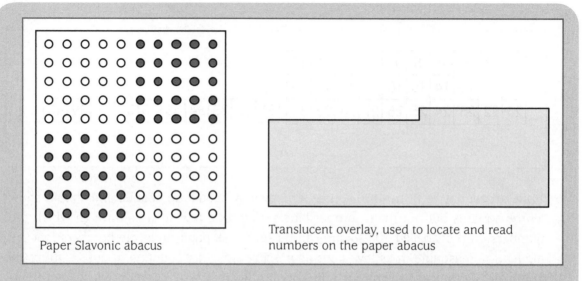

Paper Slavonic abacus

Translucent overlay, used to locate and read numbers on the paper abacus

7. Locate numbers on an empty number line. Give pupils a number below 100 to put anywhere on an empty number line. Pupils should mark on the number line the two round numbers, i.e. multiples of 10, on either side of the number.

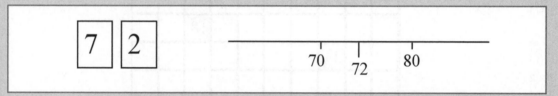

To make sure pupils understand that 100 is a multiple of 10 (as well as a multiple of 100) include several numbers in the nineties for this activity. It is equally important that pupils understand that the two 'round numbers' between which all the numbers from 1 – 9 lie, are zero and 10.

 Activities

Complements to 20

Look back at the activities on learning complements to 10, in Section 1, before trying these.

1. Give each pair of pupils two of the 10-bead strings, with which they are by now familiar from earlier activities. One pupil hides some beads in their hand while leaving others on show. It is very important that only one string is split into components: to show 6, for example, keep one whole string in the hand as well as four beads from one end of the second string; to show 16, keep only 4 beads in the hand while dangling the whole of one string and 6 beads from the other, etc. An important part of this activity is to help pupils realise that complement problems only require that one set of ten numbers is 'broken into', leaving the other decade(s) undisturbed. For this reason, it is better to use two 10-bead strings for this activity than a 20-bead string.

The second pupil in the pair must 'read' the number of beads on show, by subitising instead of counting, as far as possible, and must deduce – using knowledge of complement facts, not by counting – how many beads have been hidden.

2. Use the bead strings to reinforce the important logical idea that as one component increases, the other decreases by the same amount, and vice versa. With the two bead strings lying end to end, let pupils make a number between 1 and 20, e.g. 16. Pupils should be able to demonstrate that if they move a bead from the large group to the smaller group, one component decreases from 16 to 15 and therefore the other must increase by the same amount from 4 to 5.

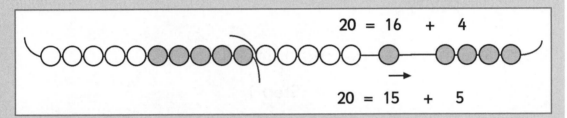

3. Give pupils enough Cuisenaire rods to make a staircase to 20, and then to add rods to each step to make a 'wall' as they did in an earlier activity in this section. Examining and discussing the wall helps pupils to understand how two components can be adjusted in opposite directions to add up to the same amount. Working from the fact that 20 = 7 + 13, we can use logic to predict how other rows in the wall are built, for example that 20 must also equal (7 + 2) + (13 – 2) which is 9 + 11, or (7 – 1) + (13 + 1) which is 6 + 14.

4. Make 'complement of 20 sandwiches' out of Cuisenaire rods. In the lid of the rods' box, have pupils set out four orange 10-rods, as shown below, leaving enough space between the layers to fit another row of rods. The teacher calls out a random number between 1 and 20. Each pupil makes that number out of the minimum number of rods, and sandwiches it between the two layers, aligning the rods at the left. Pupils must first predict, then check by measuring (again using the minimum number of rods) which number exactly fits the remaining gap. Alternatively, use a 20 cm ruler that has a special 1 cm channel to take rods or Dienes blocks for this activity.

orange	orange
orange	orange

5. The sandwich or ruler activity above represents the number 20 as a 'train' measuring 20 cm long and 1 cm high. However, it is also useful to repeat the activity with an alternative shape: a rectangle of 10 cm x 2 cm. A net for making a shallow cardboard tray in which two 10-rods fit exactly side by side can be found on the CD. 💿 When using the tray for this activity, sometimes position the tray vertically and at other times horizontally.

6. Play a brisk game of Complements Ping-Pong, for pairs of numbers totalling 20. In response to a random number between 1 and 20 being called out, each pupil in turn has to 'bounce back' the complement to 20, without pausing to calculate it. A pupil who takes too long is deemed to have 'dropped the ball', and must sit out the rest of the round.

7. Make number searches for pupils to find adjacent complements to 20, as described in Section 1 for complements to 10. Pupils can learn as much about complementary pairs when they are the ones to create the number puzzle as when they are the ones to solve it.

 Activity

Complements to larger multiples of 10

Step 1

Use a partially labelled number track where each number is represented by a 1 cm square. The track can be created by the pupils by cutting it out of 1 cm squared paper. Pupils should label the minimum number of squares that they feel comfortable with, e.g. every tenth or fifth number. Next, pupils cut the track into strips of ten numbers, and arrange the strips to form the top of a 100-square, just as they did in the earlier activity on locating and putting into context various two-digit numbers.

Step 2

Pupils generate a two-digit number by turning over two digit cards from a shuffled pack. Pupils use Cuisenaire rods to match the number, placing the rods on the 100-square. The figure below shows the number 27, with two orange 10-rods covering the top twenty numbers, and a black 7-rod covering the seven squares in the third row. Pupils must now use their complement knowledge, together with an examination of how many rows are left uncovered by rods, to find the complement to 50, i.e. the number that must be added to 17 to make 50. (See also the activity later in this section on complements to 100.)

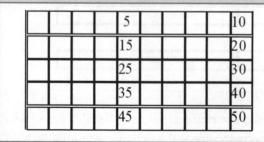 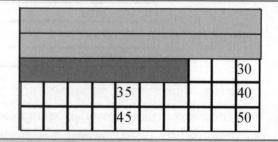

The problem posed by this activity can be recorded both as a missing-number addition, and as a subtraction sentence, e.g. 27 + ☐ = 50 and also as 50 − 27 = 23. After trying the activity for several numbers, pupils should make up at least one word problem.

Activity

Complements on a number line

Pupils draw an empty number line. Two-digit numbers are chosen by the teacher, or generated at random using dice or cards. The number is marked anywhere along the line. Pupils draw a jump on the number line towards the next multiple of 10. Pupils must label both the name of the next multiple of 10 (which they practised in earlier activities in this section) and the amount of the jump (which they should recognise as a complement fact).

This activity can be usefully extended by asking the pupils also to record the previous multiple of 10 and its distance from the target number.

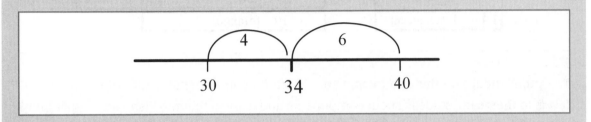

After trying this activity for various two-digit numbers, encourage pupils to answer some of the same questions again, orally, by visualising a blank number line in their mind's eye.

 Activity

Introduce bridging through 10 with Cuisenaire rods

Bridging through 10 is the single most useful mental calculation strategy that pupils can learn. Pupils will need to practise the technique in a variety of ways until they can perform bridging calculations without the help of concrete materials or paper and pencil.

Use a 10-rod sandwich to explore when to use the bridging through 10 strategy. For example, put a blue 9-rod between the two orange 10-rod layers of the sandwich. The rods now represent the starting position of any addition that begins 9 + ☐. Explore with pupils what numbers added to 9 do not require bridging (only 1 or 10) and which do require bridging (all other numbers).

10	[orange]
9	[blue]
10	[orange]

Later, substitute another rod for the blue rod, and repeat the investigation.

Here is how I might talk through an addition such as 9 + 7. *To add 7 to 9, let's set up a sandwich. We can see straight away that we will need to bridge through 10. Our first number is 9 and the complement of 9 is 1. So we need to split the second number, the 7, into 1 and what's left. Let's take a 7 and do it. When we break 7 into 1 and what's left, we get 1 and 6. The 1 will attach itself to the 9 to make 10, and 6 more makes 16. So, 9 + 7 is the same as 9 + 1 + 6, which is 16.*

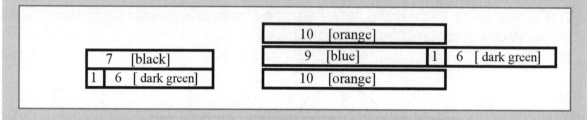

The pupil should be the one to split the 7 into its components. Quite often pupils will revert to their earliest ideas about components and tell you that the 7 should be split into 3 and 4. Your response will be that their suggestion is correct, but not helpful in this situation. Pupils may need several reminders that the split that is needed for bridging is: *the complement of the first number, and whatever is left of the second number.*

Game

Five and What's Left

A game for two or three players.

Teaching points:

◆ The game gives practice in bridging through 10.

◆ It teaches when to use the bridging through 10 strategy.

◆ It incorporates revision for the complements to 10 facts.

Equipment needed:

◆ A game board (see CD).

◆ Cuisenaire rods.

◆ A 0–9 die.

Rules:

Start with a 5-unit yellow Cuisenaire rod on a 1 × 10 cm rectangle. Players take turns to throw the die and take the rod to match the throw. If adding the two numbers (5 plus the number thrown) gives a total of 10 or less, the player cannot proceed and wins nothing on that round. If the total is more than 10, the player must use rods to explain how to use the bridging through 10 technique to find the total, and must exchange the added rod for two rods: a 5 and what's left. The player keeps the second rod – the rod representing 'what's left' – as winnings. The winner of the game is the player who has won the most after 5 rounds.

Tips:

The most valuable part of this game is the talking aloud while it is being played. To maximise the bridging practice, use a pack of digit cards in which there are more of the numbers 6–9 than of the numbers 5 and below, rather than a die.

Variations:

Adapt the game for adding onto 7 – i.e. Three and What's left (see CD) 💿 – or adding onto 6 or 8.

 Activity

Bridge through 10 on a number line

Demonstrate two slightly different approaches to bridging on a number line, and then allow each pupil to choose which way s/he will adopt and practise. Take, for example, 9 + 7.

Method 1.

Draw an empty number line. Mark 9 anywhere on the line. Bridge from the 9 to 10. Explain that we know (because we know the complements, or because we know that anything plus one is the next number) that this is a 'jump' of only 1. We need to add 7 and so far we've only added 1. Therefore we need to add 6 more. Draw a jump of 6 and label the number line. Now we can see that the answer is 16.

Method 2.

Draw an empty line. We have 9 and need to add 7. We can show this on a number line by marking the 9 and adding, or 'jumping' forward, 7. But we cannot immediately see where this lands on the number line. So, to make life easier for ourselves, we will split our addition jump into two steps and bridge through 10. The first step must be 1, because 1 is the complement of 9. We have taken care of 1 out of the 7; that leaves another six to add. Six more than ten is sixteen.

The advantage of the second method over the first is that the whole question is notated on the number line immediately, making it less likely for pupils to lose their place and forget what they are supposed to be doing. The disadvantage is that it can look messy, especially if pupils leave insufficient space for a jump to be subdivided.

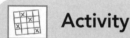 Activity

Practise bridging and reinforce the commutativity of addition

Arrange pupils into pairs or into two groups. Give all pupils the same addition problem for them to solve on a number line, using a bridging strategy as described in the activity above. Half of the pupils are asked to solve the problem as it is given, e.g. 9 + 7, while the other half must switch the order of the numbers before proceeding, e.g. 7 + 9.

Number line work is a good opportunity to reinforce the commutative property of addition, and this activity promotes discussions between pupils about whether one approach is better, or faster, than another. For example, the number line calculation for 7 + 9 is just as easy, or as difficult, as 9 + 7, as shown below. However, the same is not true when one addend is a two-digit number (see next activity).

Activity

Bridge through multiples of 10 on a number line

Set up additions where a one-digit number is added to a two-digit number. Make the connection with earlier work explicit, i.e. that the second addend must again be split into *a complement and whatever is left*, just as before. What is new is that now larger multiples of 10 are used as stepping stones on the way to the final total. Encourage pupils to set out their calculation on an empty number line, as before. For example:

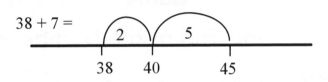

After trying a few additions like this, challenge pupils to solve the same questions without paper and pencil, by visualising the number line in their mind's eye.

Game
Race along a Number Line and Bridge

A game for two players.

Teaching points:

◆ The game focuses on the bridging through 10 strategy.

◆ It gives practice in using an empty number line for addition.

◆ It gives practice in visually estimating the size of numbers below 10, relative to a whole 10.

◆ It makes pupils notice which sums need the bridging through 10 strategy and which do not.

Equipment needed:

◆ A paper copy of the game board (see CD) 💿 with pencils.

◆ A die. A 10-sided die makes for a faster game than a 6-sided die.

Rules:

Players have their own number lines and agree on a round number to start (not always zero). They mark the next four multiples of 10 on their lines, then take turns to progress in jumps along the number line according to the throw of a die. Players only win points if they bridge through a multiple of 10. The game ends as soon as one player reaches, or passes, the end of his/her line. The score is one point for finishing first, and two points for each time the bridging technique was used (so 9 is the maximum score).

Tip:

Insist on clear and neat recording, with the amount of the addition labelled in or above each jump, and the running total marked beneath the number line at the end of each jump.

Game

Race to the End of the Number Line

A game for two players.

Teaching points:

◆ The game practises the use of an empty number line for addition.

◆ It brings into sharp focus the difference in quantity between a ten and a unit.

◆ It gives practice in visually estimating the size of one in relation to ten.

◆ The game teaches that adding single ones or whole tens does not require the bridging through 10 strategy, even though adding a 10 always crosses a decade boundary.

Equipment needed:

◆ A paper copy of the board (see CD) with pencils.

◆ A die with three sides labelled '+1' and the other three labelled '+10'.

Rules:

Players take turns to throw dice and to race along number lines, recording their turns as jumps, and labelling their lines as they move forwards.

Tip:

It is best to vary the length of the number lines and the spacing of the numbers on the line each time the game is played, so that pupils begin to see that number lines are flexible and can represent whatever sequence of numbers they wish.

Activity

Complementary addition, or subtracting by adding

Step 1

Remind pupils of the work they have already done on complementary addition with small numbers (see Section 1). Ask pupils to explain it back to you, and to each other, first by using counters and then on a number line.

The key idea is that the number to be subtracted is taken away from the beginning of the array of counters, or from the start of the line, so that the whole calculation moves in the forward direction.

Remind pupils that they can physically cross out the amount to be subtracted on a number line beginning at zero, and only begin to use an empty number line that does not start at zero when they are completely convinced that both representations model the same problem. For example:

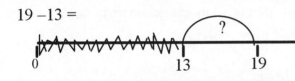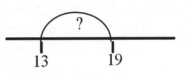

$19 - 13 =$

Step 2

Give pupils lots of practice in using number lines for problems like the above, where both the numbers in the question have two-digits, but where the answer is below 10.

Step 3

Ask pupils to use their number line solutions to the problems in the previous step, and to rewrite the problems as an equalising (or difference) problem, using the missing-addend notation, e.g. $13 + \boxed{} = 19$. This part of the activity reinforces the relationship between addition and subtraction. It also shows pupils that, because work on a number line is in the forward direction, there is no need for arrows on the jumps or operation signs for the quantities.

Step 4

Give pupils the same kinds of problems as above, but without paper and pencil. Pupils must practise putting an empty number line in their mind's eye and working forwards along it. You should provide the actual question in writing, as it might put too great a strain on a pupil's memory to have to keep hold of the numbers of the question, while mentally calculating the answer. This kind of activity should not be timed. However, these problems can be answered in only two steps, so check that pupils who are very slow are not finding the solution by counting in ones.

 Activity

Complementary addition for subtracting round numbers

This activity provides an important transition between the previous activity (beginning to use complementary addition) and the next activity ('harder' complementary addition). This activity teaches pupils to subtract multiples of 10 in one go where possible, or, later, in two steps where bridging through hundreds is necessary.

Step 1

Use Cuisenaire rods, or Dienes blocks, in conjunction with an empty number line.

Set up subtraction problems for pupils to answer, where the minuend (the first number) is not a round number, e.g. 75, and the subtrahend (the number to be subtracted) is any multiple of 10 that is easy to subtract from the tens digit in the minuend, e.g. 40. Other example are 72 – 60, 86 – 20, 99 – 50, 264 – 30, etc.

Step 2

Have pupils build the first number out of concrete materials, and model the subtraction by covering the number of tens in the subtrahend with a translucent overlay (e.g. a piece cut out of a plastic wallet). The answer can clearly be seen as all the tens that have remained uncovered, together with all the units that have remained untouched.

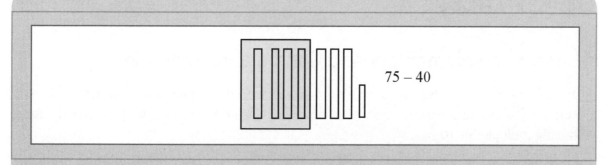

Step 3

Pupils draw two number lines and mark both numbers on them. On the top number line, the pupil makes one bridging jump for the tens, talking it through aloud, e.g. *I have 4 tens and I'm moving forwards to 7 tens, that means I move 3 tens which is 30*, or once they are more practised, *40 to 70 is 30*. Pupils draw a second jump for the units and say: *70 to 75 is 5*. Immediately underneath, the pupil repeats the subtraction but drawing only one jump and saying aloud: *from 40 to 75 is thirty . . . five*.

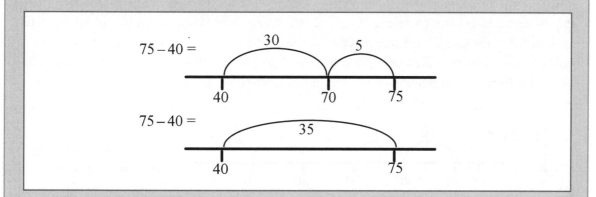

Step 4

Pupils practise these kinds of subtractions mentally, by visualising a number line.

Activity

Harder complementary addition on a number line

Do not attempt this activity until pupils are secure with the earlier activity in which there were only one-digit answers, and with the previous activity in which they practised subtracting multiples of 10.

The technique is basically the same as any other complementary addition, but the aim of this exercise is to encourage pupils to minimise the number of steps. For example, a subtraction such as 76 – 28 can be done in two steps.

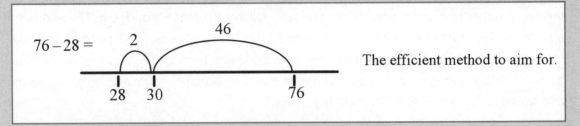

The efficient method to aim for.

Pupils who can get the correct answer only by doing the calculation in lots of small steps should be given plenty more practice of the earlier activities. The benefit of using a number line is completely lost if the pupils need to add too many jumps to reach the solution, or if they end up doing lots of counting in single units of one or ten.

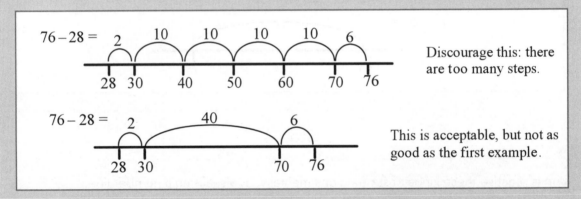

Discourage this: there are too many steps.

This is acceptable, but not as good as the first example.

The hardest subtractions involve successive bridging: through a multiple of 10, and through a multiple of a 100. It can be done efficiently on a number line, but only if pupils can subtract a round number of hundreds from a three-digit number, e.g. 364 – 200.

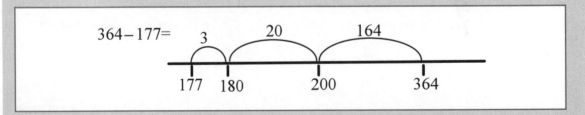

My general rule is that if the number of steps on a number line exceeds four, the number line method should be abandoned in favour of written column addition or subtraction.

Activity

A flexible approach to partitioning

Dictate a two-digit number between 20 and 100 for pupils to build out of Cuisenaire rods. Pupils must find as many different ways of partitioning the number into two components as possible, by moving only one rod at a time from one component group to the other. For example, 35 is built with 3 orange 10-rods and one yellow 5-rod, and so can be partitioned into 30 + 5, into 20 + 15, and into 10 + 25. This activity reinforces an understanding of partitioning that will be useful for subtractions requiring decomposition.

As an extension of this activity, challenge pupils to determine whether different solutions are possible by moving, say, all the tens before the units rod, or altering the order of the movements in other ways. Pupils will find that different solutions are not possible for the same number. This extension activity, therefore, also reinforces the commutative principle of addition, i.e. that 20 + 15 is the same as 15 + 20.

 Activities

Explore partitioning methods for 2-digit mental additions

These activities should not be tried until pupils have some understanding of place value (see the activities in Section 3). Note that in contrast to column addition, the actual values of the numbers are kept throughout, i.e. 20 remains twenty, never two (although it could be thought of as two tens).

1. Add a two-digit number to another two-digit number by partitioning, using rods.

   For example: 45 + 23. Make 45 out of four orange 10-rods and a yellow 5-rod. Make the number 23, separately, out of two orange 10-rods and a light green 3-rod. Push the orange rods together into one group and name the quantity (*sixty*), then do the same for the units and name the running total: *sixty . . . eight*.

   When adding two numbers whose units add up to more than 10, there is an extra step. For example: 45 + 28. Make the numbers out of rods as before, and combine the tens together, naming the amount (*sixty*), then do the same for the units and name the amount (*thirteen*), finally teach pupils to say aloud not the sum, but just the running total: *sixty . . . seventy . . . three*.

2. Show pupils how to record the mental partitioning method informally. Take an example that has been set out with concrete materials, like the one above, and show how both the two-digit numbers have been split into tens and units, so that the original question

45 + 23 has been turned into the question 40 + 5 + 20 + 3 (do not write this down; explain orally while pointing to the relevant rods). Combining the tens before combining the units results in a question that can be expressed as 40 + 20 + 5 + 3 (again, do not write this down, but explain *orally*). Now show the two best ways of writing and reorganising the sum as follows:

$$\textbf{45} + \textbf{23}$$
$$40 + 5 + 20 + 3$$
$$60$$
$$8 \qquad = 68$$

or

$$\begin{array}{c} 60 \\ \textbf{4 5} + \textbf{2 3} \quad = 68 \\ 8 \end{array}$$

Pupils should try both ways a few times, before settling on the one they like best.

3. Practise the above activity including some additions that require carrying. For example:

$$\textbf{36 + 88}$$

$$30 + 6 + 80 + 8$$
$$30 + 80 + 6 + 8$$
$$110 + 14$$
$$\textbf{Answer: 124}$$

$$\begin{array}{c} 11\ tens = 110 \\ \textbf{36 + 88} = 124 \\ 14 \end{array}$$

 Activity

Teach an alternative written method for column addition

Teach pupils a non-standard column method that avoids the two main problems that pupils have with the standard algorithm: it (practically) eliminates 'carrying', and the sum can be worked from left to right, i.e. starting with the largest values, just as for mental addition.

The method works by collecting a subtotal 'under the line' for each column, before adding the sub-totals to produce the final solution. For example:

$$
\begin{array}{r}
36 \\
+ \quad 88 \\
\hline
\text{tens} \quad 110 \\
\text{units} \quad 14 \\
\hline
124 \\
\hline
\end{array}
\qquad
\begin{array}{r}
473 \\
+ \quad 102 \\
56 \\
\hline
\text{H} \quad 500 \\
\text{T} \quad 120 \\
\text{U} \quad 11 \\
\hline
631 \\
\hline
\end{array}
$$

Activity

Show how to avoid decomposition in subtraction

This activity shows pupils how much easier it is to use complementary addition than to use columns for those subtraction problems that would otherwise require decomposition.

Set up some subtraction problems where there are one or more zeros in the minuend (the first number), e.g. 200 – 56 or 104 – 78. Demonstrate both ways of solving, first by column arithmetic, then by complementary addition on a number line. For example:

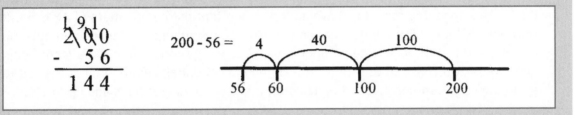

Give pupils practice in solving subtractions that normally require 'borrowing' or decomposition (whether or not the numbers contain zeros), on a number line as well as in columns. Many pupils will find the number line method much quicker and easier, especially if they have already had plenty of practice using number lines to support or record mental calculations. Pupils who prefer to use the standard written algorithm for these difficult subtractions can still use complementary addition to check their answers.

 Activities

Complements to 100

Complements to 100 should be given lots of practice because knowledge of these facts will be needed for calculations to do with money and metric measurements. Of course, the five complement facts to 10 must be known by heart first.

1. Build Cuisenaire rods on top of a Dienes 100-block or in a shallow cardboard tray that measures 10 cm × 10 cm (see CD for net). 🔘 This is an extension of the earlier activity in this section on complements to multiples of 10.

   Have the pupils generate a random two-digit number by throwing a set of tens and units dice. Pupils take the Cuisenaire rods to match the dice throw and arrange them on top of the 100-block, aligned at the left. Pupils then cover the remaining space on the block with one coloured rod and some orange 10-rods. For example, if 40 and 6 were the dice throws, the rods would look like this:

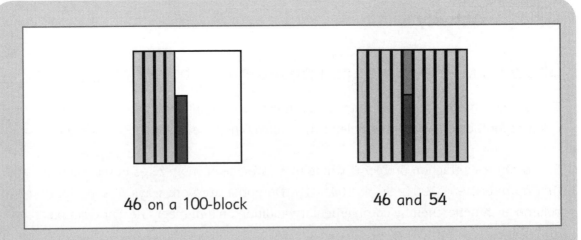

46 on a 100-block   46 and 54

Pupils now 'read' the rods they have added to find that the complement of 46 is 54. It is important for pupils to notice that only one of the ten orange rods that could build up to 100 has been 'broken' into components. *Nine* orange rods remain, the *tenth* being built out of two coloured unit rods. This is the crucial understanding that is needed to avoid the very common error when children make complement pairs add up to 110.

Remind pupils that rods are tools for building mental models, not for getting answers mechanically, and challenge them to answer some of the same problems without using rods (or fingers), but perhaps while having a 100-block in view.

2. Use a Slavonic abacus and later a paper abacus. Both of these are described in the earlier activity in this section on locating two-digit numbers and putting them into context.

As in the activity above, pupils generate random two-digit numbers using tens and units dice. With all the beads on the abacus aligned on one side, have the pupils slide as many beads as are shown on the dice to the other side. Make sure the pupils do not count in ones, but slide whole tens across, and then all the units in one sweep. The pupils can now find the complement to 100 by reading the beads that have not been moved.

As before, draw the pupils' attention to the fact that on nine of the abacus rows, the beads remain in unbroken groups of ten; it is only one row where the group of ten has been split into two components, which are, of course, complement pairs.

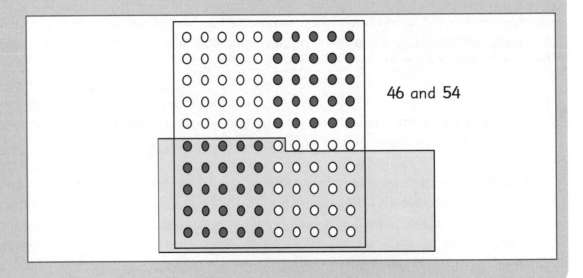

46 and 54

If the pupils are using a paper abacus, show them how to use the translucent overlay to cover just the right number of dots, without counting in ones. The overlay on a paper abacus can be used in any orientation that suits the pupils: horizontally from the top down or from the bottom up, or vertically from the left or from the right.

3. Complementary addition on a number line. Earlier activities have described complementary addition on a number line in great detail, so pupils should be able to use the method for complements to 100 without any special introduction.

   Give pupils two-digit numbers, or have them throw dice to generate numbers. Pupils should only draw the number lines if they feel they need to. If they can find the answer by visualising a number line in their mind's eye, so much the better. Pupils must practise doing the calculation in only two steps: first to the next multiple of 10, and then in one jump to 100, as in the example below.

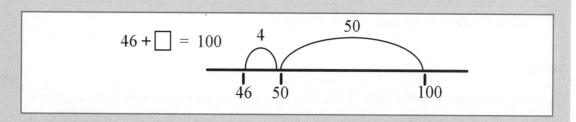

4. Give children practice in solving complements to 100 problems against the clock. They should be able to choose whichever of the above methods they like best to support their mental thinking. Challenge pupils to see how many sums they can do in one minute, or time them, giving them the opportunity to beat that number or that time on the next occasion. An example of a worksheet can be found on the CD.

5. Give pupils money problems of the 'how much change' sort, telling them explicitly to use their knowledge of complements for the solutions. An example of a worksheet can be found on the CD.

6. Tracking complements to 100. Make a worksheet on which are several rows of two-digit additions, some of which add up to 100 and others that add up instead to 90, 99, 101, or 110. Pupils, working as fast as they can, against the clock, must circle only the pairs of numbers that add up to 100. The top row of the tracking worksheet might look like this:

   28 + 82   56 + 44   39 + 71   24 + 66   15 + 85   77 + 33.

Game
Keep the Change!

A game for two players or a small group.

Teaching points:

◆ The game gives practice in complements to 100.

◆ It shows pupils that it helps to know complement facts when solving problems about money.

◆ It gives practice in making amounts out of coins, and in counting amounts in coins.

Equipment needed:

◆ Coins.

◆ A pair of tens and units dice.

Rules:

Each player starts the game with £5 (or €5) so that they can 'go shopping' to buy five (virtual) items. They throw both dice, five times in all, to see how much each item costs. After buying each item, they keep the change from £1 (or €1). The winner is the player with the most money at the end of the game.

Tips:

The £1 or €1 coins will probably need to be made of plastic or card, but try to provide real coins for the lower denominations if possible, as it makes the game more exciting for the children to collect and count real money.

 Activity

Learn the doubles up to 10 + 10

The doubles facts to 5 + 5 should already be known by heart (see Section 1).

Have pupils make a doubles pyramid out of Cuisenaire rods, like the one shown below. It can also be drawn onto squared paper, preferably 1 cm squared paper, so that the rods fit exactly on top. Make sure that when pupils build the models out of pairs of rods, or when they draw them, the line of symmetry is clearly visible. Use a mirror in the middle to reinforce the symmetrical structure, as this will help pupils think of doubling as 'twice as much' instead of the less useful 'add one more group'.

Show pupils exactly how they can use this visual model to find doubles facts: each double is visibly 2 more than the previous fact – one on each side of the pyramid – and 2 less than the next double fact. The hardest doubles to remember are, traditionally, 8 + 8 and 9 + 9. However, children who can easily visualise the pyramid and know that 9 + 9 is the step before 10 + 10, are able to reason back from 20.

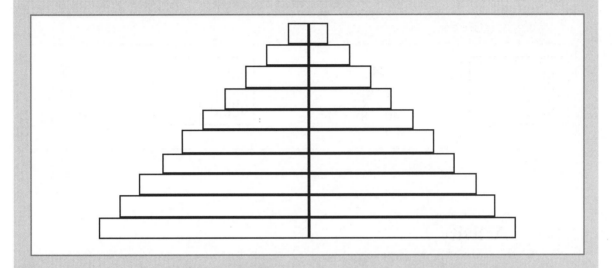

Pupils who find it difficult to visualise this model may use a bridging through 10 technique instead. For example, 'double 8' becomes 8 + 8, which becomes 8 + 2 + 6 on a visualised number line, to give 16.

Have pupils 'read' the rows of the pyramid, using the words 'double' or 'twice'.

 ## Activities

Practise and extend the doubles facts

1. Give pupils dice to generate random numbers to double: a normal die will give practice up to 6 + 6 and a 1–10 die will give practice up to 10 + 10.

2. Play a game of Doubles Ping-Pong. The teacher calls out a number between 1 and 10. Each pupil in turn has to 'bounce back' the double as quickly as possible. A pupil who takes too long is deemed to have 'dropped the ball', and must sit out the rest of the round.

3. Use rods to demonstrate to pupils how their existing doubling knowledge can be extended to larger numbers. Note that pupils must have some understanding of place value first (see Section 3). For example, for double 24, make the number out of rods and put it in a tens-and-units formation on one side of a piece of paper which has been folded, or clearly marked, in half.

If necessary allow the pupils to make the number again on the other half of the paper, but as soon as possible encourage pupils to imagine that the fold line is a mirror so that they can visualise the doubling, without having to actually see two groups of rods. At this stage, show pupils how to make an informal notation, like the one shown in the figure below, with separate arrows from each digit.

Next, do the same for numbers where the units are between 5 and 9, e.g. double 36.

Activity

Halving is the opposite of doubling

Halving is much harder than doubling, quite apart from the problem of halving odd numbers. The main difficulty is that halving does not declare itself in the same way as doubling. For example, all pupils can see that 19 + 19 is a doubling question even if they do not know how to find the answer, whereas 38 – 19 does not signal to the solver that there is any doubling or halving involved.

Therefore, a good way to start halving practice is to set up a situation where pupils have to find half of a number that they have only recently doubled, and vice versa. An exercise that helps pupils connect the two ideas and the two procedures can be found on a worksheet on the CD.

Activity

Find half of round numbers

Use Cuisenaire rods to find half of round numbers. Start with numbers that have an even number of tens. Move on to numbers that have an odd number of tens, which will require much more practice. At first, allow the pupils to physically split the odd orange rod into two yellow rods. After a while pupils should be able to find the answer by just looking at the rectangle of long rods and introducing judicious spacing, as shown overleaf. Finally, give pupils problems to solve mentally, without rods.

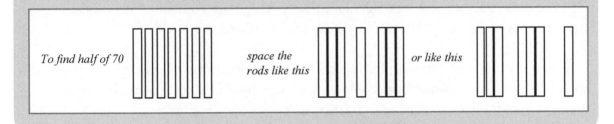

 Activity

Function machines for doubling and halving

Introduce pupils to the idea of a function machine: a 'machine' that performs the same, pre-agreed, operation on any number that enters the machine.

Introduce a doubling machine by drawing something very simple, like the example below. Make sure that the operation the machine performs, and the direction of movement from left to right, are both very clear. Label the machine either '× 2' or 'double'.

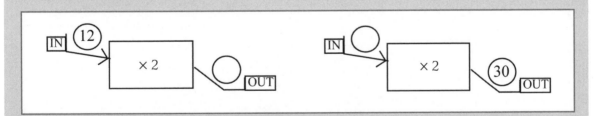

Pupils are given numbers that sometimes go into the machine, and sometimes come out of the machine. Repeat the activity for halving machines, to emphasise the connection between doubling and halving. To avoid one of the more common problems, do not ask pupils to halve odd numbers yet.

Activity

Use reasoning to find near-complements and near-doubles

Remind pupils of the key reasoning idea that you will already have introduced to them in previous activities: that when a number has two components, as soon as one component is increased or decreased by an amount the other component must be adjusted by the same amount in the opposite direction, if the total is to stay the same.

This work can now be extended to using complement facts and doubles facts with larger numbers. For example, because you know 20 + 80 = 100, you can work out what to add to 22 to make 100, without treating it as a new and separate problem. A doubles example might be: work out 16 – 7 from your knowledge that double 8 is 16.

Put one of the known complements or doubles facts up on the board, and ask pupils to find and write down some near-complements and near-doubles questions that can be derived from these facts. Pupils swap papers and answer each other's problems.

Two worksheets that are designed to give pupils practice in reasoning from complement facts and doubles facts can be found on the CD.

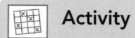

Activity

9 is almost 10

Using Cuisenaire rods, show the following two ways of adding 9 to a number, for example, 6 + 9. Put a 6-rod and a 9-rod end to end. In the kind of addition that has been described in earlier activities, pupils measure the total length starting with an orange rod from the left. This time, however, put the 10-rod immediately under the 9-rod.

In language that should already be familiar to them, show pupils that because the 9 is being increased by one unit to 10, the other component must be decreased by one unit, in this case from 6 to 5. So, the problem 6 + 9 becomes 5 + 10.

The other, slightly different, way is to put an orange 10-rod under the 9-rod so that the extra unit is sticking out. This time the explanation points out that because 10 is one more than 9, adding 10 will overshoot the target by one unit, which must then be adjusted by 1 in the opposite direction. So, the problem 6 + 9 becomes 6 + 10 – 1.

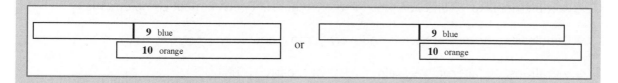

After making sure pupils understand the logic of both these slightly different methods of adding 9, pupils should be allowed to choose only one of the methods for themselves. Set up lots of problems for adding 9 to two-digit and then three-digit numbers for pupils to practise their own chosen method.

The techniques can also be adapted to + 99: either pupils can decrease the first addend by 1 so that they can use the 1 to combine with 99 to make 100 (pupils quite enjoy the idea of 'pinching' 1 from one number and attaching it to the other); or pupils can add 100 to the first addend and then subtract 1.

Activity

The Basic 8 strategies

The 'Basic 8' strategies are the most useful, and most important, mental arithmetic strategies for addition and subtraction. It is often a relief to pupils to learn that there are only eight strategies they need to know for basic competence. What is more, they already know them.

Details of all these strategies can be found in earlier activities, both in this section and in the previous section. What is new about this activity is that the pupils are being explicitly told about the Basic 8 strategies and are taught to focus on when each strategy is helpful. The Basic 8 strategies are:

◆ Plus or minus 1

◆ Plus or minus 2

◆ Plus or minus 10

◆ Complements to 10 and near-complements (alternatively 'almost complements')

◆ Doubles and near-doubles (alternatively 'almost double')

◆ 9 is almost 10 (alternatively 'almost 10', or 'nearly 10')

◆ Bridging through 10

◆ Complementary addition (alternatively 'subtraction by adding').

Make cards to give to pupils, or have the pupils make a set of cards for themselves, with the strategies written on them, one strategy per card. See the CD 🖭 for cards that you can photocopy and distribute to pupils. I prefer to use ten cards for the eight strategies, but you could combine the 'complements and near complements' and the 'doubles and near doubles' if you prefer the logic of eight cards for eight strategies.

Present the cards to the pupils one at a time (probably not all at the same lesson), reminding them that they already know the strategy, and invite examples from the group to demonstrate the strategy. Collect some examples on the board. For example, give all the pupils the card labelled 'plus or minus 1', explain the sign ±, and say: *Who remembers this strategy? How can we find the answer to a number plus or minus one? Give me an example of a number question that asks us to add or subtract one.* After collecting a number of suitable examples, wipe them off the board before asking pupils to write one example for themselves on the back of their card, so that they will be able to remember what the label on the front means.

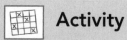 **Activity**

Identify which strategy works best in different situations

Together with the pupils, examine a page full of easy mixed addition and subtraction problems to give children practice in determining when any of the Basic 8 strategies can be helpful. On the CD, you will find a worksheet called *Which Strategy?*, that can be adapted by including all the Basic 8 in the list of known strategies, and by including larger numbers in the addition and subtraction problems.

Pupils can win a point for identifying a good strategy, and another for a correct answer. Remind pupils that counting up or down in ones is not considered to be a good strategy unless there are only one or two steps. Note that some problems can be solved by more than one good strategy, e.g. the answer to 60 – 31 could be found because it is a near-double fact or by complementary addition (which requires knowledge of complement facts, therefore 'using complements' cannot be named as a third strategy). A pupil who identifies both strategies, and gives the correct answer of 29, can score three points.

SECTION 3

Place value

Overview

This third section collects together the activities that help teach the concept of place value, i.e. that the value represented by a numeral depends upon its position within a number. This concept cannot be left until all the activities in the previous two sections have been completed, but must be introduced alongside the earlier work on basic calculations.

Place value is an abstract idea that many children find confusing. An understanding of the place value system is best cultivated by activities that focus on the notion of exchange.

In addition to the regrouping and conversion ideas that are fundamental to the concept of place value, pupils must learn that in the decimal system the base is 10 and that the column positions therefore represent powers of 10.

A note about the threefold nature of the column labelling system

Most children are first introduced to single-digit numbers, and, as they grow older, to two-digit numbers (which we teach them to call tens and units) and then to three-digit numbers (introducing the hundreds) and later still to four-digit numbers (introducing thousands). This gradual introduction leads many children to assume that every column in our place value system has a completely new name. This misconception is at the root of the very common mistake in which pupils 'lose' or merge one or more of the columns, especially those denoting tens of thousands and hundreds of thousands.

It is, therefore, important to tell pupils explicitly that entirely new labels are given, not to every column, but to every group of *three* columns. Each new 'family' of place values – ones, thousands, millions, billions, etc. – consists of subsections of units, tens and hundreds, each in their own column. Thus, multi-digit numbers have (starting at the right): units, tens and hundreds of *ones*, then units, tens and hundreds of *thousands*, then units, tens and hundreds of *millions*, etc.

My experience is that a clear explanation of the threefold logic behind place value column labels often comes as a complete surprise and revelation to students of all ages.

What are the main problems?

◆ Confusing the absolute value of the numbers 1–9 with the symbolic value of numerals in multi-digit numbers.

◆ Not appreciating that our place value system has a decimal structure, i.e. it is based on powers of 10.

◆ Being unaware of the threefold pattern of 'units, tens, hundreds', or that it is a repeating pattern.

◆ Not understanding how zero works as a place holder.

◆ Having no feel for the actual value of large numbers.

◆ Making no connections between place value work and mental calculation.

◆ Not recognising that multi-digit numbers can be partitioned into tens and units in more than one way.

How to help

◆ Do not rush the early work with concrete materials. Progress in very small steps. Revisit early activities often.

◆ Do not insist that everything is recorded in writing. Practical experience comes first.

◆ Remember that concrete materials are best used to help build cognitive models and should not be used simply to find an answer mechanically.

◆ Let the pupils manipulate the concrete material themselves, to explore new ideas. Do not restrict the use of apparatus to demonstrations only, or just to illustrate a written algorithm.

◆ Use continuous materials that showcase ten as a single unit, in preference to discrete materials that require sequential counting and consequently encourage pupils to see 10 only as a group of ten ones.

◆ Use proportional concrete materials such as Cuisenaire rods or Dienes blocks, before using more abstract representational materials such as a spike abacus, colour-coded chips, or money.

◆ Use concrete materials before diagrams. Use pictures and diagrams as a transitional stage between concrete and abstract work.

◆ Emphasise the repeating pattern of units, tens and hundreds (see the overview to this section). In column work always set out columns in groups of three. For example, even when working with numbers of four digits, show six columns (i.e. including all three of the thousands columns). Similarly, use three or six, never four, spikes on a spike abacus.

◆ Be explicit about what is happening at every step. Encourage pupils to talk aloud about what they are doing and why. When you are doing the talking, vary your vocabulary.

◆ Use hypothetical questions to encourage visualisation and mental work.

◆ Explain to pupils explicitly that place value is a kind of shorthand to save time. Experiment with longhand writing of numbers and informal jottings to highlight the efficiency of the standard place value system.

◆ Play games that help teach place value. Set games for homework practice.

◆ Spend at least as much time on subtraction as on addition. Concrete activities and games that help illuminate decomposition are especially valuable.

◆ Teach pupils how to split numbers into components in a variety of ways, e.g. 32 = 2 + 30 and also 12 + 20.

◆ Be explicit about the connection between the mental calculations that pupils are already familiar with and the more condensed notation and procedures of column arithmetic.

◆ After showing pupils different ways of splitting and recombining two-digit numbers, allow each pupil to settle on only one or two methods to practise and adopt.

Activities

Exchange units into tens

1. On different occasions, use different objects that you designate as 'units'. From a large heap of units, pupils must sort out ten and find ways to keep the ten in a separate group, e.g. by using saucers, boxes, small transparent plastic bags, rubber bands, or sticky tape. The objects could be bricks, cubes, hairpins, lolly sticks, plastic shapes, games tokens, counters, beans, beads, pebbles, nuggets, buttons, paper-clips, shells, straws, toothpicks, spaghetti shapes, bolts, strips of paper, lengths of ribbon, cards, pencils, etc. At the end of the activity, each pupil must say how many tens s/he has and therefore how many units are contained in the bundled groups.

2. Set up activities like the one above, where there is a banker who will exchange ten units for a packaged ten, and where children can accumulate items according to the throw of a die, or the spin of a spinner. After practising this activity with some of the objects suggested above, pupils can also exchange ten white Cuisenaire cubes for an orange rod at the bank, or ten unit cubes for a Dienes long, or ten pennies for one 10p coin, or ten 1 cent coins for a 10 cent coin.

3. Set up a bank for making exchanges like the activity above, but where the exchange is not measurable. Instead, it is the result of a previously made agreement. For example, pupils can exchange ten small shirt buttons for a fancy button, or five dull-coloured counters for a shiny one, or five beans for a small marble and ten beans for a large marble. This activity emphasises that exchange is about equivalent value.

Activities

Concrete counting on place value mats

Cuisenaire rods are excellent for place value work if you use only the white and orange rods (except for step-counting). Dienes blocks, or other base-10 materials, are just as good (again except for step-counting).

You can enlarge, photocopy and laminate the mats provided on the CD. But it is also useful practice for pupils to make their own mats. Note that the hundreds column must be at least 10 cm wide to accommodate base-10 material, and that it is logical to make each column the same width.

In the following counting activities, do not always start the count at zero or one.

1. *Count up and exchange.* A pupil takes or makes a place value mat (see CD). The pupil takes one white cube at a time out of the Cuisenaire box and puts it on the mat,

keeping a count of the running total. As soon as there are ten white cubes they must be exchanged for an orange 10-rod which is put in the tens column. The pupil explains the exchange procedure, and the reason for it, aloud.

2. *Decomposition is the inverse of exchange.* Reverse the process described above, so that a pupil starts with a random amount on the mat made up of white and orange rods and returns one cube at a time to the Cuisenaire rods box, counting down as s/he goes, and explaining aloud the decomposition procedure when a 10 must be exchanged for units.

3. *Group work, counting up.* A small group uses one place value mat (but it is very important that all members of the group are looking at it the right way up). Pupils take it in turns to add one white cube to the group's collection and announce the total so far. The pupil who puts a tenth cube onto the unit side of the mat is responsible for making the exchange and explaining aloud what is happening and why. The size of the groups should be planned so that the exchanges do not always fall to the same pupils. Do not always start the count at one.

4. *Group work, counting back.* Reverse the process described above so that members of a group are removing rods one at a time and counting backwards. Ensure that it is not always the same person who has to perform and explain the decomposition procedure.

5. *Hundreds, tens and units.* All the activities above can be adapted for a three-column mat (see CD). 💿 The counting up and down is now done in tens, so the unit column will remain empty throughout. The exchange, and decomposition, procedures must be explained aloud.

6. *Cross-counting.* Pupils in a small group use one three-column place value mat between them, with all viewing the mat the right way up. Just as in the activities above, pupils take turns to add one rod to the mat, announce the accumulated total, and perform any exchange or decomposition that is necessary on their turn. What's new in this activity is that a randomly timed noise, like a teacher's hand-clap, becomes the signal for the pupils to change from counting in ones to counting in tens, and then back again at the next clap.

7. *Cross counting up and down.* Extend the above activity by having someone call out what kind of counting the group must perform, and changing the instructions frequently: counting up or counting down, combined with counting in ones, tens or hundreds. It is very useful for pupils to be able to do this concretely before they are expected to cross-count abstractly without supporting materials.

8. *Use money on place value mats.* The activities above can be performed with money, instead of rods, on the place value mats. For two-column work use 1p and 10p coins (or 1 cent and 10 cent coins) and count in ones, or use a 1–3 die to accumulate different amounts at each step. For three-column work use £1 (or €1) coins in the hundreds column in conjunction with a 1–10 or a 1–20 die. As already mentioned, it is important for the pupils to articulate aloud exactly what is happening when exchanging coins and moving them from one column to another on the place value mats.

Game
Magic 10s

This is one of Prof. Sharma's games, for two or three children (see his 1993 articles on the *Place Value Concept*).

Teaching points:

◆ The game teaches that ten units, when grouped together, form a single unit of 10 times the value, i.e. that 10 is ten ones, and at the same time, is also one ten.

◆ It teaches that quantities set out in a tens and units pattern can be determined without having to start counting from one.

◆ It reinforces the connection between our spoken names for two-digit numbers and their tens-and-units structure.

Equipment needed:

◆ A place value mat for each player, showing two columns labelled 'Tens' and 'Units'.

◆ Unifix cubes, i.e. unit cubes that can be attached together end to end.

◆ A die or spinner.

Rules:

Players take turns to throw the die or spin the spinner, and accumulate single cubes on the units side of their mats, according to the number thrown. The rule is that 10 is the magic number, so cubes can only be clicked together when there are ten of them. As soon as a ten is made it is moved onto the tens side of the mat. Play continues for a certain number of turns, or a certain length of time, before the winner is found, or until one player reaches a target number, say 30.

Tips:

It is a good idea if each player calls out how much s/he has accumulated so far after every turn. At first play with a 1–3 die or spinner; later with larger numbers, e.g. 1–6 or 4–9 dice or spinners.

 Activities

Make a 20-step staircase and explore the 'teen' number names

1. Have the pupils make a staircase from 1 to 10 out of Cuisenaire rods and then extend the staircase to 20. This activity, which is described and illustrated in Section 2, highlights the way that the 'teen' numbers are constructed out of tens and units.

2. Use the staircase to help pupils connect the spoken names for the numbers 11–19 with the actual values. Tell pupils explicitly that the 'teen' numbers are irregular. The words

eleven and twelve seem to have no connection with the tens-and-units combinations, while in the numbers 13 to 19 there is a discrepancy between the order in which we write the digits and the order in which we hear or say them. By contrast, the numbers above 20 are more consistent because tens come first in both spoken and written formats.

 Activity

Cover 20

Make a shallow tray measuring 10 cm by 2 cm out of card (see CD for net) for each pupil. The pupils' aim is to fill their tray with rods. Pupils throw a 6-sided die, take a single rod to match the throw, and place the rod in the tray. As the total value of the rods approaches 10, pupils (usually) have to exchange a new rod for two smaller rods in order to fit them into the tray. Pupils then swap their collection of smaller rods for a single orange 10-rod. They must talk through all the decompositions and both of the exchanges needed to fill the tray.

Game
Race to Cover 100

A game for two or more players.

Teaching points:

♦ The game focuses on the principle of exchange that underlies place value.

♦ It provides a concrete model of 100 that pupils can later connect to the abstract 100-square format.

Equipment needed:

♦ A tray to fill (see CD 💿 for net) for each player, or a Dienes 100-block each as a base to cover.

♦ Two 1–6 or 1–10 dice.

♦ Cuisenaire rods, including 10 orange rods for each player.

Rules:

Players take turns to throw the dice and take as few rods as possible to match their throw (i.e. not a pile of ones). Players put the rods in columns, working from left to right across the 100-square. As each column fills, pupils may have to exchange a single rod for two smaller rods, so that each column is filled before a new column is started. Any whole column of rods is exchanged for an orange rod. Pupils keep a running total, both spoken and written, of how much they have after each turn. The winner is the first to fill their tray, or square, with ten orange rods.

Game

Four Throws to Reach 100

This game for two or more players is proposed by Ian Sugarman in the 1997 book *Teaching and Learning Early Number*, edited by Ian Thompson.

Teaching points:

◆ The game helps build a sense of the magnitude of numbers up to 100.

◆ The game teaches base-10 place value.

◆ It shows the connection between column value (e.g. 3 tens) and quantity value (30).

Equipment needed:

◆ A board (see CD) or a place value mat for each player.

◆ White and orange Cuisenaire rods, or units and tens from a set of Dienes blocks, or 1p and 10p coins.

◆ A 1–6 die.

Rules:

Players take turns to throw the die. No player may miss a turn and the round ends when each player has had four throws. Each player must decide immediately after each throw whether to take that number of single units or that number of tens. Any player whose total goes over 100 is out. The winner of the round is the player whose total is nearest 100. Play several rounds, or play for 5 minutes, to find the overall winner of the game.

Variation:

Use tens and hundreds blocks, or equivalent coins, for a target of 1000.

Activities

Make and read numbers made of Cuisenaire rods or base-10 materials

Cuisenaire rods can be supplemented by 10 cm x 10 cm x 1 cm flat blocks in plastic or wood, to represent 100. Large cubes to represent 1000 can also be bought, but are expensive. You could make cardboard 1000-cubes, and even glue ten such cubes together to make a 10,000 'long'.

1. Give pupils two-digit numbers to make with concrete materials. At first, the numbers can be built on place value mats, to get pupils used to the idea that the tens are grouped together at the left (and not arranged into a long train, as they were in earlier activities with smaller numbers). Later, numbers can be made without the mats. Pupils should read the number they have made, and can also record it on paper, as shown below. Give plenty of practice with the teen numbers as well as the larger numbers.

2. Pupils pick two digit cards from which they must build the larger of the two possible two-digit numbers. When the rods are laid out, the pupil takes the card representing the tens digit and puts it on the orange rods, and puts the unit card as close as possible to the white rods. The pupil then repeats the exercise with the same cards now arranged to make the smaller 2-digit number.

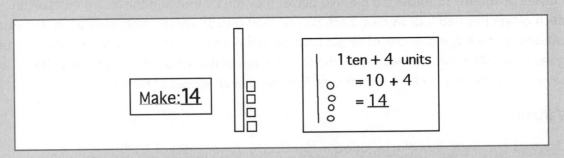

3. Pupils take a small pile of mixed white and orange rods. They must arrange them in a tens-and-units pattern and read the pattern to find the total value of the rods.

4. In any of the activities above, it is useful for the teacher to ask hypothetical questions – such as *What if you had . . . one more ten*, or *one less unit* – so that pupils learn to visualise the concrete materials and manipulate the quantities in their mind's eye.

5. The four activities above can be repeated with three-digit and four-digit numbers.

6. Pupils make multi-digit numbers in groups, with one pupil responsible for the tens, another for the hundreds, etc. All pupils read the number. Pupils swap roles after a few numbers.

Games

Dice and spinner games

Dorian Yeo gives a good selection of place value games in her book *Dyslexia, Dyspraxia and Mathematics* (2003). Most of them are played on place value mats with concrete base-10 materials. Spinners, labelled 'ones' and 'tens', or 'H', 'T' and 'U', are used on their own or in conjunction with dice to produce instructions to add, or subtract, amounts from one column at a time. The most valuable aspect of these games is the focus on *change* in the values of the concrete materials, rather than on a static amount. An integral and important part of each game is that players record quantities in columns at the end of every turn.

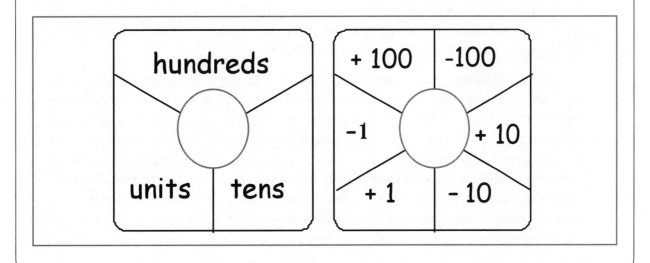

Activities

Practise subtraction and decomposition with concrete materials

1. Have the pupils build any two-digit number below 25 on a place value mat using Cuisenaire rods or Dienes or similar base-10 materials. Use a 1–3 die to decide how much is to be subtracted at each turn. The pupils must say, before touching any of the materials, whether an exchange will be necessary. At every decomposition, the teacher supervises the exchange, and encourages the pupils to talk through what they are doing and why. Pupils must write down what remains after each subtraction.

At the end, pupils should be asked to look back at this list of numbers, and deduce the die throw. Pupils can be asked to write down some of the subtractions both as horizontal equations and as vertical subtractions in columns.

It is really important not to let pupils carry out this activity without supervision. (After all, if they can do it without any muddle on their own, they do not need to practise the activity at all.) Here is how to manage the all-important exchange: the 10-rod should be taken off the mat, and placed in a designated exchange area, e.g. the lid of the box of rods, or a piece of paper. The ten units are counted up or lined up and measured alongside the ten, and then taken by the pupils, as a whole group, back to the mat. The units should be put initially into the tens column, or along the line that separates the tens from the units column, and then immediately moved into the units column. During all these procedures, the pupils should commentate in detail about every action.

2. Repeat the activity described above, starting with two-digit numbers above 25 and using a die showing larger numbers, e.g. 0–9 or 4–9 .

3. Repeat the activity with three-digit numbers between 100 and 200, on a place value mat, with a 0–9 die. Later, use larger numbers and a 1–20 die.

4. Repeat the activity with three-digit numbers, but use a die to show how many tens, not units, are to be subtracted. It is now the hundreds that will be decomposed and exchanged.

5. Try some of these activities using money instead of base-10 blocks or rods.

All five activities can be adapted into games where pupils compete with each other.

Game

Spot the Decomposition

A game for two players, or a solitaire activity.

Teaching points:

◆ The game familiarises pupils with the (sometimes inverted) vocabulary of subtraction.

◆ It teaches pupils not to assume that subtraction means a smaller amount taken away from a larger one, e.g. when taking 6 from 23 vertically, not to fall into the common error of reversing the units and finding 6 − 3).

◆ It gives practice in identifying the situations where decomposition will be necessary.

Equipment needed:

◆ Cards, made by the teacher, on which are written various subtraction problems, some of which require decomposition to solve and others that do not. Present some problems vertically, some horizontally, and some using words, as in the examples below.

Rules:

Players race to sort all their cards into two piles: 'decomposition needed' or 'no decomposition'.

| 18 − 5 | 23
− 6 | Take 14
away from
16 | 27 minus 11 | 41
subtract 7 | 135 − 22 |

Activities

Use a spike abacus

There are so many sources for ideas on using a spike abacus to teach place value, that I do not detail any here. However, there are some important considerations to bear in mind.

Never use four spikes of the abacus. Start with two spikes for two-digit work, followed by three spikes for three-digit work. Use six spikes for four-digit, five-digit and six-digit numbers. This is so as to emphasise the threefold nature of our place value system, as explained at the start of this section.

Abacus work is more abstract than work with rods. It may be helpful to use different coloured beads for each place value spike at first. Abacus work makes a useful transition between concrete and pictorial or diagrammatic work.

Be aware that some children who struggle with arithmetic have directional confusion. It is therefore crucial for pupils to have a front view of the abacus at all times.

Game
Win Counters on a 100-Square

A game for two or three players.

Teaching points:

◆ The game highlights the place value structure of the numbers below 100.

◆ It familiarises pupils with the 100-square format.

Equipment needed:

◆ A 100-square, i.e. a paper square showing all the numbers from 1 to 100 (see CD).

◆ 17 counters, each of a size to cover one of the squares.

◆ Two 0–9 dice.

Rules:

Players sit facing the 100-square and place the counters at random over the square, so that each counter covers and hides one number. Players take turns to throw both dice. They may arrange the digits in whatever order they choose to form a two-digit number. The player tries to match a number hidden by one of the counters by adding (or subtracting) either 1 or 10 to (or from) the number created on the dice. If successful, the counter hiding that number can be removed from the board and kept. The winner is the player who has won the most counters.

Tips:

Do not allow players look underneath the counters to see the hidden numbers. Because the game gets slower as there are fewer counters on the board, play for a certain number of turns, rather than until all the counters have been won.

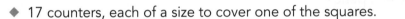

Game

Race through a 100-Square

A game for two or three players.

Teaching points:

◆ The game highlights the place value structure of the numbers below 100.

◆ It familiarises pupils with both the horizontal and vertical formats of the 100-square (see CD).

Equipment needed:

◆ An empty paper 100-square and pencils.

◆ A token for each player.

◆ A pair of tens and units dice.

Rules:

Players take turns to throw the dice and to move their tokens accordingly. At each turn, players must write the correct number in the blank square on which they land. The first player to reach, or pass, 100 is the winner.

Tip:

Before the game starts, players must decide if the numbers will run from left to right in rows or from top to bottom in columns. Choose the alternative format for the next game.

Activities

Practise adding and subtracting 10 and 100

Set up paper-and-pencil exercises that give pupils practice in adding and subtracting 10. If you see pupils using their fingers to count they will need more time exploring the earlier activities that use concrete materials, before returning to these abstract exercises.

1. Written addition problems might look like this: ☐ + 10 = ☐, where dice can be used to provide random numbers to go in either the first, or sometimes the second, box. An activity sheet of addition problems like these can be found on the CD.

2. Written subtraction problems might look like this: ☐ – 10 = ☐. Again, vary the exercise by sometimes giving a number to be put in the first box and sometimes in the second box. An activity sheet of subtraction problems like these can be found on the CD.

3. Later, extend this abstract work to adding and subtracting tens and hundreds from three-digit numbers.

Game
Steer the Number

This is another Ian Sugarman game for two or three players from the 1997 book *Teaching and Learning Early Number*, edited by Ian Thompson.

Teaching points:

◆ The game teaches place value.

◆ It teaches adding and subtracting multiples of 10 from two-digit numbers.

◆ It shows how two-digit mental calculations can be achieved in steps, one 'column' at a time.

◆ It gives practice in using a calculator.

Equipment needed:

◆ A tens-and-units place value mat.

◆ Base-10 materials, e.g. Cuisenaire orange and white rods, or Dienes blocks.

◆ A pack of cards with one each of the numbers 1–99 (or a list of ten unique two-digit numbers for each player).

◆ A calculator.

Rules:

Each player takes ten cards from the shuffled pack, or is given a list of ten random two-digit numbers (numbers that no other player is given). Players win a point when one of these numbers is created during the course of the game. A random number is chosen as a starting number and is built from concrete materials on the place value mat. Each player in turn makes one change to the quantity on the mat, by either adding or subtracting any number of 10-rods *or* unit-cubes, and announcing what they are doing while they do it. For example: *I'm taking away two tens, so now there is . . . left.* After the action, the same player uses the calculator to record the addition/subtraction. Players may not add or subtract an amount that would require adjustments to both sides of the mat (i.e. a player cannot add more than 7 to 2, or subtract more than 2 from 2); nor is any player allowed to miss a turn. At any time that the mat contains the exact number on a player's list, whether by their own actions or their opponents' actions, the player crosses the number off the list and wins a point. The winner is the first player to have made all ten numbers and won 10 points.

Tips:

There is more luck involved when each player keeps their list of target numbers hidden from the others. On the other hand, it can be more fun for players to see all the target numbers and to try and think up what strategy will maximise their own chances of winning.

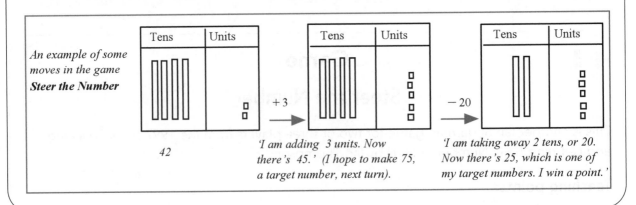

An example of some moves in the game **Steer the Number**

42

$+3$

'I am adding 3 units. Now there's 45.' (I hope to make 75, a target number, next turn).

-20

'I am taking away 2 tens, or 20. Now there's 25, which is one of my target numbers. I win a point.'

 Activity

Transform a two-digit number in two steps

Pupils will find this abstract activity more meaningful if they have previously played the Steer the Number game above.

Pupils make a starting number by taking two digit cards and arranging them in whichever order they prefer. A second two-digit number is made by throwing tens and units dice, i.e. no choice is given about the order of the digits of this second number. The pupils must say, and then record on paper, how to change the first number into the second, in two steps: the first step will alter the tens and the second step will alter the digits. For example, to change 28 to 76:

28 → 76   *Add fifty, subtract two.*   28 + 50 = 78   78 − 2 = 76

Activity

Teach the threefold repeating pattern: units, tens and hundreds

Make explicit to pupils that numbers are written in groups of three: first units, tens and hundreds of *ones*, then units, tens and hundreds of *thousands*, then units, tens and hundred of *millions*, etc. (See the introduction to this section.)

Teach pupils to make and label place value columns in sets of three, like those below. Use thick lines to emphasise the threefold grouping. After writing the labels as shown, pupils might like to put into brackets the final 's' of the 'millions' and 'thousands' labels and the word 'ones' (and half of the word 'tens') since these do not form part of the spoken labels.

Reassure pupils that, once they can read and write three-digit numbers, they can read and write any number.

Millions			Thousands			Ones		
Hundreds	Tens	Units	Hundreds	Tens	Units	Hundreds	Tens	Units

Millions			Thousands			Ones		
H	T	U	H	T	U	H	T	U

 Activities

Explore place value as a shorthand

1. Dictate any four-digit number whose digits range from 1 to 9 (but not zero) for the pupils to write down as follows: numerals are to be used for the digits but words (or letters for the contraction 'ty' for the word 'ten') are to be used for the values. For example, for the dictated number '2375', the pupils must write:

   2 thousand 3 hundred and 7-ty 5

   Pupils should turn the page sideways – landscape format – so that the whole number can be written on a single line. Pupils now use a highlighter to write over the digits, and at the end of the line write the whole number in digits, which they copy from the board.

   2 thousand 3 hundred and 7-ty 5 = 2375

Continue to dictate other four-digit numbers in the same way. After a while ask pupils what they notice. If necessary, draw their attention to the fact that the digits are always in the same order, and that therefore the words 'hundreds' or 'thousands' are implied even when they are not written out, just as the word 'units' is implied but not spoken in the numbers below 10.

2. Have pupils write a four-digit number using only digits but with all the values shown as multiplications of powers of ten. For example, the number 2375 is written:

$$(2 \times 1000) + (3 \times 100) + (7 \times 10) + (5 \times 1)$$

Even without the brackets, this is an unnecessarily long way of writing a four-digit number, even though it is mathematically correct. The convention of having columns denoting the value of digits is therefore revealed as a useful shorthand.

 Activities

Read and write multi-digit numbers

1. Show pupils how the place value columns work, starting with three-digit numbers that contain no zeros at first, e.g. 365. Repeat the same digits in the thousands columns, e.g. 365 365, and explain how to read this new number, pointing to the column headings as you do so. Repeat the same digits in the millions columns and explain how to read this new number, 365 365 365. Give lots of practice in reading a variety of three-digit, six-digit and nine-digit numbers, before introducing numbers with zeros and numbers of other amounts of digits.

2. Invite a pupil to label nine columns and to write a nine-digit number with one digit in each column. The number is hidden under a sheet of paper. Other pupils in the group must read the number aloud, while the sheet of paper is moved to the right in stages, so that three new digits are revealed at each stage.

3. Show pupils how to insert commas between each triple-column grouping of H, T, and U. Emphasise that the groups of three must be counted from the right, or from the decimal point, and only then can the number be read, starting from the left. Commas should not be too large, must always sit on the line, and should never be able to be confused with a decimal point.

4. Give pupils practice in adding and subtracting 10 or 100, from four-digit, five-digit and six-digit numbers.

Activities

Build up large numbers, one column at a time

1. Use a page with clearly marked column headings as a base sheet, and some transparent overlays. Deconstruct a three-digit number onto three separate transparent overlays, and then put the overlays one over the other, on top of the headed columns, to reconstruct the number. For example, for the number 825, make one overlay showing 800, another showing 20 and a third showing 5. While you do this, remind pupils of the work they have already done building three-digit numbers from concrete materials. When the number is reconstructed, by putting the overlays on top of each other, the last two digits seem to be superimposed onto zeros (the number will be easier to read if you exaggerate the size of the zeros slightly). Eva Grauberg, from whose book *Elementary Mathematics and Language Difficulties* (1998) this activity is taken, suggests that pupils can find it helpful to see numerals superimposed onto zeros in this way.

| *Numbers written on transparencies* | 800 | 20 | 5 | HTU 825 |

2. Repeat the activity with numbers that include zero as a place-holder.

3. Repeat the activity with numbers larger than three-digits.

4. Repeat the activity without the overlays, but simply writing a number on paper, by starting with the largest value and writing new digits inside the zeros as lesser values are added to complete the number. Pupils should be encouraged to copy this procedure themselves. Later pupils can write 'invisible' zeros, without actually marking the paper, to remind themselves of the real value of each digit as they combine digits to build a multi-digit number.

 Activity

What is the value of . . .

Step 1

Build a three-digit number out of base-10 materials. For example, the number 241.

Step 2

Write the number so that each digit is in a separate, labelled, column.

Step 3

Use both the concrete and the written representations to answer such questions as:

What is the value of the 2? [Answer: 200.]

What value has the 4 in the number 241? [Answer: 40.]

How many tens are shown in the tens position? [Answer: 4 tens.]

Note that these questions are place value questions.

Step 4

Contrast the above place value questions with the following, and demonstrate the difference with concrete materials:

How many tens are there in 241? [Answer: 24.]

How many hundreds are needed to build 241? [Answer: 2.]

How many units are in 241? [Answer: 241.]

Note that these questions are really division questions, but of a kind that can be easily answered by simply looking at the digits and their positions. This happens because the division required to answer these types of questions is division by a power of 10, and our place value system is a decimal one, i.e. it is based on powers of 10.

Step 5

Repeat this exercise without the concrete materials, using written notation alone. At first, have pupils always label the place value columns; later do without the labels. Give plenty of practice in answering both types of questions, and – crucially – in distinguishing between the two types.

Step 6

Ask both types of questions about numbers larger than three-digits.

Game
Two-Digit Sequences

This game, based on one devised by Prof. Sharma, is for two players (see his 1993 articles on the *Place Value Concept*).

Teaching points:

◆ The game focuses on place value.

◆ It teaches that the leftmost digit (the one in the tens position in a two-digit number) is the most important signifier of value.

◆ It gives practice in ordering (putting into sequence) two-digit numbers.

◆ It makes explicit how many whole tens are contained within a two-digit number.

◆ It helps connect the spoken words we use for two-digit numbers with their written notation.

Equipment needed:

◆ A pack of digit cards, including zeros (four cards each of the numbers 0–9).

◆ Paper and pencil for each player.

Rules:

Each player takes two cards from the top of the shuffled pack, and lays the two cards on the table in whichever order s/he chooses. Players write down the number they make as a simple tens and units statement. For example, if the cards are 2 and 4, the player might choose to position the card showing 4 to the left of the 2, and write *4 tens + 2 units = 42.* Players repeat this four more times with new cards, until each player has made five two-digit numbers and written five number statements.

   Players now rearrange their two-digit numbers so that the digit cards are lined up in two columns, and the five numbers are sorted into a sequence, in descending order. Each player checks the other's sequence. If the cards are not correctly sequenced, the opponent is allowed to remove any cards in the wrong order, taking care to remove the minimum number of cards necessary to leave a descending sequence. Players score one point for each ten contained in the correctly ordered numbers.

Tips:

The writing is an important part of this game, because it reinforces the fact that position determines value. It also provides a handy memo of what the numbers were, in case the cards get mixed up during the sequencing activity.

Variation:

Play with three cards to make three-digit numbers. Score one point for each hundred.

Game
Three-Digit Sequences with the Focus on Tens

This game, for two players, is a version of the one above, but focuses on tens within a three-digit number.

Teaching points:

◆ The game teaches place value.

◆ It teaches that to determine value one must examine the digits from left to right.

◆ It gives practice in sequencing three-digit numbers.

◆ It makes explicit how many whole tens are contained within a three-digit number, as opposed to just identifying what digit lies in the tens place (two questions that are very often confused).

Equipment needed:

◆ A pack of digit cards, including zeros (four cards each of the numbers 0–9).
◆ Paper and pencil for each player.

Rules:

Each player takes three cards from the top of the shuffled pack, and lays them on the table in whichever order s/he chooses. Each player writes down the number s/he has made as a simple hundreds, tens and units statement. For example, if the cards are 2, 5 and 4, the player might choose to position the card showing 5 to the left of the 4 which in turn is to the left of the 2, and write *5 hundreds + 4 tens + 2 units = 542*. Players repeat this twice more with new cards, until each player has made three 3-digit numbers and written three number statements.

Players rearrange their three-digit numbers so that the digit cards are lined up in three columns, and the three numbers are sequenced in descending order. The score is calculated as one point for each ten that goes to build up each number, e.g. in the example above the score is 54, because there are 54 tens in 542.

Tips:

One of the most important teaching points of this game is to get children to understand the difference between looking to see what digit is in the tens place in a multi-digit number (i.e. 4 in 542), and understanding how many whole tens are contained within a multi-digit number, or how many tens would be needed to build the number out of tens and units (i.e. 54 in 542). This is often a major source of confusion, and is best explained by using base-10 concrete materials at first, as described in an earlier activity, followed by games such as this.

Game

Place Value Boxes

A game for two or more players.

Teaching points:

◆ The game teaches place value in large numbers.

◆ It gives practice in making connections between column value (e.g. 3 tens) and quantity value (30).

Equipment needed:

◆ A pack of digit cards made of four each of the digits 0–9.

◆ Paper and pencil for each player.

Rules:

Each player draws six boxes with a very small gap between each set of three. Each box represents one place value column. One card is dealt to each player on each round. The player must choose which box to copy the digit into. After six rounds each player will have a six-digit number, which they must read aloud. Decide before the game starts, whether the winner will have the largest or the smallest number.

Variation 1:

Give each player one set of the digits 0–9, shuffled and face down. Players turn over the top six cards from this pack, one at a time, as above. This variation involves rather more strategy than the basic game.

Variation 2:

At the start of the game, agree on a target number for all players to aim for. A six-digit round number is best. The winner is the player who comes closest to the target.

Tips:

You can see in the illustration below what the game will look like, but resist the temptation to photocopy the box format. Pupils will learn much more by having to sketch their own boxes each time they play.

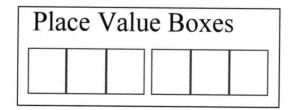

Game

Calculator Skittles

A game for any number of players.

Teaching points:

◆ The game teaches place value in large numbers.

◆ It also teaches how to use a calculator for subtraction.

Equipment needed:

◆ A calculator for each player.

Rules:

Players choose any four-digit number that does not include a zero, and enter it into their calculator. They may repeat digits if they like. The teacher calls out any number between 1 and 9 for the players to 'knock down'. Each player who has that digit on their calculator screen is now allowed to perform one, and only one, subtraction on the calculator, the aim being to replace that digit with a zero. Any pupils who mistake the place value of the digit and do not manage to 'knock it down' to zero must live with their mistake and continue with whatever number their calculator now shows. The teacher continues calling out random digits until one or more of the players achieves a zero display on their calculator and is awarded a point. Players then choose new numbers and a new round begins. The winner is the player with the most points after a certain period of time.

Variation 1:

Instead of letting children choose, players get allocated a four-digit number by dealing digit cards or throwing dice.

Variation 2:

Use numbers that have more than four-digits.

Tips:

The teacher can use a die, or a pack of digit cards, to generate the random numbers between 1 and 9. If pupils write down the number they started with, they can demonstrate at the end exactly how they arrived at zero.

Activity

Partition numbers into tens and units in various ways

Make a two-digit number out of rods or base-10 materials, e.g. 52 made of five longs and two cubes. Earlier activities have shown pupils that this number can be split into tens and units and read as five tens and two units, or as 50 + 2. The focus of this activity is to show that other splits are also possible.

Place the tens on one small piece of paper and the units on an adjacent piece, so that you are creating two visual groups. One at a time, move one 10-rod from one group to the other, to show that just as 52 can be made of 50 and 2, it can also be made of 40 + 12, or 30 + 22, or 20 + 32, or 10 + 42.

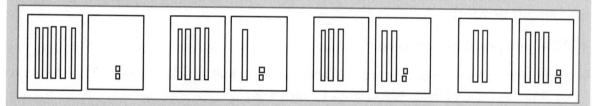

This concept of partitioning the tens in different ways, while keeping ideas of place value firmly in mind, is a necessary step before pupils can really understand decomposition in subtraction. It will also prove very useful for short division.

When pupils are ready, repeat the activity for three-digit numbers.

Finally, practise partitioning numbers in various ways without the concrete materials.

 Activity

Split off the 'teen' numbers

This is an extension of the activity above, but with the focus on splitting off the numbers between 10 and 19, which is what needs to happen during decomposition for subtraction.

Make two-digit, and later three-digit numbers, by throwing dice or dealing digit cards. Pupils must split this number into the 'teen' number, and whatever is left. The process can be written down either as a standard addition sum, or using an informal triangular notation, as shown below.

$$79 = 19 + 60$$
$$\text{or } 79 = 60 + 19$$

$$79 \quad \text{or} \quad 79$$
$$\bigwedge \qquad \qquad \bigwedge$$
$$19 + 60 \qquad 60 + 19$$

Game
Jump 10

A game for two or more players.

Teaching points:

◆ The game teaches how to use number lines to record simple additions.

◆ It shows that numbers that are ten apart share the same digit in the unit position.

◆ It teaches how to relate vertical place value thinking to horizontal mental calculation processes.

Equipment needed:

◆ Paper and pencil for each player.

◆ A die with half the faces labelled '+1' and the other half labelled 'Jump 10', or a coin to be spun with one of these labels stuck to each side.

Rules:

Each pupil draws their own number line and takes turns to throw the die and record the instructions on their number line. Pupils announce their running total at the end of each turn. Pupils race to have the highest score after a certain number of turns, or a certain period of time.

Variation 1:

Pupils can race to be the first to hit a pre-agreed target number.

Variation 2:

Pupils can play this as a solitaire game. First they determine a target number, perhaps by throwing dice, and then they try to predict how many throws it will take them to reach the target.

Variation 3:

Change the instructions to read '+10' and 'Jump 100'.

Variation 4:

Start at an agreed number and work backwards. In this case the die must be labelled '−1' and 'Jump back 10'. Players must start their recording at the rightmost end of the number line and draw the jumps backwards, towards the left, including arrows on the jumps to show the direction of play.

Tips:

Pupils should turn their pages sideways, landscape fashion, so that they can fit as many jumps as possible onto a single line. Do not allow pupils to 'jump 10' by counting up in ones or by bridging though 10.

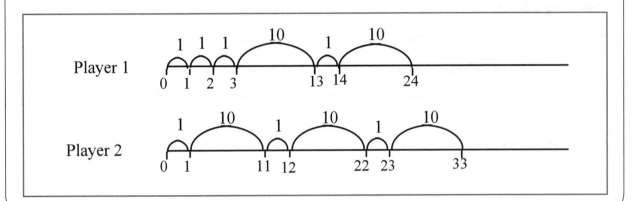

Activities

Locate any number on a number line

1. This activity can also be found in Section 2. Here, pupils are focusing on how the tens-and-units structure of a two-digit number relates to the sequential number line concept. Pupils take a 2-digit number and mark it anywhere on an empty number line. Pupils should mark on the number line the two round numbers (multiples of 10) on either side of the number.

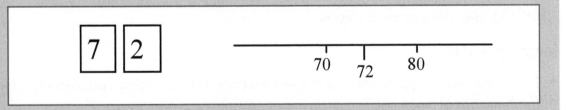

2. Repeat the activity for three-digit numbers. Pupils must now mark the multiples of 10 on either side, and also the multiples of 100 on either side. Sometimes include numbers where the adjacent multiple of 10 is also the adjacent multiple of 100, e.g. 295 or 603.

These activities could lead into teaching about how to round numbers to the nearest 10 or 100.

Game

The Six-Card Rounding Game

A game for two, three or more players.

Teaching points:

- The game teaches place value.

- It focuses on rounding two-digit numbers to the nearest 10.

- It gives practice in rearranging and reading different combinations of digits.

Equipment needed:

- A pack of digit cards made of four cards of each of the numbers 0–9.

Rules:

Players are dealt six cards each, which they turn face up and rearrange as three 2-digit numbers. The aim is to make numbers which, when rounded to the nearest 10, are consecutive multiples of 10. Two consecutive round numbers score 2 points; three consecutive round numbers score 5 points. For example, a player dealt 1, 1, 5, 6, 7 and 7 could make 56 (rounding to 60) and 71 (rounding to 70) for 2 points, or 51 and 61 (rounding to 50 and 60) for 2 points, or 71 and 76 for 2 points. However, the same player could score 5 points for making 61, 71 and 75. The winner is the player with the highest score after five rounds.

Game

The Rounding Challenge

A game for two, three or more players.

Teaching points:

- The game teaches place value and gives practice in rearranging and reading different combinations of digits.

- The game focuses on rounding two-digit numbers to the nearest 10.

Equipment needed:

- A pack of digit cards made of four cards of each of the numbers 0–9.

Rules:

As in the game above, players are dealt six cards each, which they turn face up and rearrange as three 2-digit numbers. The aim, as above, is to make numbers which, when rounded to the nearest 10, are consecutive multiples of 10. A player who succeeds with the six dealt cards will score 5 points. A player who cannot manage this may take another card from the top of the pack, and tries again to make three 2-digit numbers that round to consecutive round numbers (leaving one card unused), to score 3 points. If an eighth card is needed to succeed, the score is 1 point. The winner is the player with the highest score after five rounds.

Variation:

Players are dealt nine cards to create three 3-digit numbers that are each rounded to the nearest 100, aiming for three consecutive multiples of 100.

 Activity

Teach × 10 and ÷ 10 as a shift between columns

Use base-10 concrete materials on place value mats to show multiplication and division by 10. For example, if you start with three units, and multiply by 10, each of the three units becomes a ten, so the result is three tens, whose proper place is in the next section to the left, the tens column.

When these multiplications are recorded, make explicit to pupils how the digits have moved one column to the left. It is not true that you 'add a zero', because adding zero leaves numbers unaltered. What actually happens on paper is that the digit shifts into the next column, and a zero is needed to hold the place (in this example the units place), to record the fact that a column shift has occurred and to indicate the new value of the digits.

Before recording each multiplication on paper, use a transparent overlay on a place value recording sheet with labelled columns, and slide the overlay so that the digits visibly move from one column to the next. Have pupils articulate what is happening to the base-10 materials on the place value mat, and how this connects to what is happening to the digit(s) on the plastic overlay.

Take care when practising division not to create numbers with decimals before the pupils are ready for them.

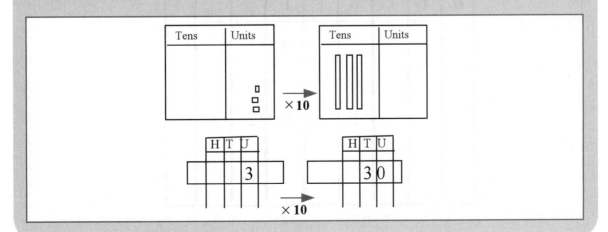

Activity

Extend place value thinking to decimals

Introduce decimals as an extension of the place value system.

Demonstrate with concrete materials how the value of the units changes tenfold with each column: moving from right to left the values increase by 10 times the amount, or moving from left to right the values become a tenth of what they were. Remind pupils of the three-fold recurring pattern of place value headings. Demonstrate how the shapes of the base-10 materials also have a threefold recurring pattern: cube, long and flat. Explain that the same repeating patterns continue into the decimal columns.

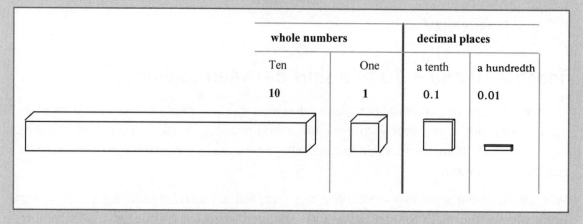

whole numbers		decimal places	
Ten	One	a tenth	a hundredth
10	1	0.1	0.01

When talking about decimals, enunciate very clearly so that pupils can hear the difference between tenths and tens, and between hundredths and hundreds. Use fraction notation, rather than lower-case letters, to label the decimal columns, as shown below.

Use headed columns like these to practise reading, writing and ordering decimal numbers. On top of the thick line separating the whole numbers from the fractional parts of the number, encourage pupils to mark an exaggeratedly large, or brightly coloured, decimal point.

Thousands			Ones			Decimals	
H	T	U	H	T	U	$\frac{1}{10}$	$\frac{1}{100}$
					4 • 5		
			1	0	6 • 2	5	

Activity

Connect decimal place value notation to money

Remember that most children first meet decimal notation in relation to money and prices.

Use labelled columns to read and write amounts of money. Have pupils put various prices that include both pounds and pence in ascending or descending order. Pupils should first read the amounts as money and then reread them as plain decimal numbers.

Make explicit to children that money is always written with two decimal places, even when the second decimal place is a zero. By contrast, in all other quantities, only zeros that act as place-holders need be written: i.e. the zero at the end of 9.0 is as superfluous as the zero at the start of 09.

Another important difference to teach children is that only in money may we express the digits beyond the decimal point as if they were tens-and-units, e.g. six pounds *twenty-five*, but six point *two five*.

SECTION 4

Times tables, multiplication and division

Overview

Trying to learn times tables can be a nightmare for dyscalculic pupils. They have to expend an enormous amount of time and effort to memorise what, for them, is one meaningless string of words after another, only to find that they cannot access any fact from the middle of the sequence on its own but must recite the whole chant again from the very beginning to reach an answer. Even worse, they often find that the act of learning a new table seems to wipe clean all memory of a previously learned table.

Learning tables by heart is so difficult for dyscalculic learners that I believe it should not even be attempted. Pupils are much better off learning to understand what multiplication means and how tables are constructed, so that they can derive any multiplication fact by logic and reasoning. Pupils should either be given enough time to find an answer by working from first principles, or should be given a tables square from which they can copy any answers they need immediately.

Pupils can be helped to see how numbers are built up out of equal sized groups by using appropriate visual models, the best of which is the area model of multiplication and division. In the early stages of teaching multiplication and division, the area model can be constructed from Cuisenaire rods or Dienes blocks arranged into a rectangular array. At a later stage the same concept is represented by diagrams of rectangles that are sketched to help support the pupils' mental calculations. After plenty of practice, pupils learn to visualise a rectangular area and manipulate it in their mind's eye. Pupils will first need to be reasonably proficient in step-counting and bridging techniques, both of which have been covered in the first two sections of this book.

What are the main problems?

◆ Being unable to memorise and recall the multiplication tables facts by heart.

◆ Having such a hazy or muddled understanding of the concepts of multiplication and division that, when their memory fails, pupils have no idea how to work from first principles towards a solution.

◆ Finding it difficult to grasp the idea of working with equal sized sets, possibly due to a persistence in seeing numbers as collections of single units, rather than as a group bonding to form one larger unit.

◆ Being unlikely to notice patterns until they are explicitly pointed out.

◆ Having such a weak number sense that there is no realistic possibility of estimating whether any multiplication or division answer is reasonable.

◆ Not yet having mastered some of the necessary mathematical pre-skills, such as efficient mental addition (that does not rely on counting in ones) or a basic understanding of place value.

How to help

◆ Give pupils practice in step-counting.

◆ Give pupils practice in simple grouping of small quantities.

◆ Use appropriate concrete materials that will help build cognitive models. Discrete material, such as counters, should give way very quickly to continuous materials, such as Cuisenaire rods.

◆ Let the pupils manipulate the concrete material themselves. Continue to offer concrete materials until pupils are ready to work with drawings and sketches instead, during their progression towards purely abstract work.

◆ Teach the area model of multiplication.

◆ Show pupils how diagrams, particularly sketches of rectangles, can clarify thinking about multiplication and division.

◆ Encourage pupils to talk aloud about what they are doing and to use their own words to articulate what a problem means and how it might be solved.

◆ Make sure all the foundation techniques are understood and have been thoroughly practised:

- basic mental addition techniques, such as bridging through 10;

- complementary addition to solve subtractions;

- a basic understanding of place value and columns;

- how to partition and recombine numbers into components;

- place value multiplication and division by 10.

◆ Teach division at the same time and alongside multiplication, from the very beginning. Teach in a way that reinforces, again and again, the connection between multiplication and division.

◆ Teach division as the inverse of multiplication, but do not present division as repeated subtraction. Instead, present both multiplication and division as repeated addition of equal sized groups. Only the point of view is different: division focuses on the groups (how many groups, or how many in each group) that build up to certain number, while multiplication focuses on the total quantity that is built from groups.

◆ Point out to pupils the patterns that multiples create. Encourage pupils to explore the patterns using concrete materials as well as using pictorial representations.

◆ Play games that teach and practise multiplication and division facts. Send games home to be played with an adult, as an alternative to written homework.

◆ Explore the language of multiplication and division. For example, what does 'times' mean, what is the difference between 'divide' and 'divided by', etc.

◆ Limit the amount of memorising to a minimum number of key facts.

◆ Teach explicitly how to derive new facts by logic and reasoning from known facts.

◆ Minimise the number of strategies and procedures that a pupil is expected to know. When there are several possible strategies, allow pupils to make individual choices about which one they would prefer to learn and to practise.

◆ Allow dyscalculic pupils to use a tables square for all work that is not directly testing their knowledge of multiplication facts.

◆ Make word problems an integral part of the teaching. Encourage pupils to make up their own problems, located in real and everyday situations.

◆ When taking pupils beyond the basic tables facts, e.g. to multiplying two-digit numbers together or to short division (both of which are beyond the scope of this book), teach the box or grid method of recording, which is related to the area model of multiplication.

 Activities

Build small numbers out of equal-sized groups

As a preliminary to these activities, ask your pupils to use counters or glass nuggets to show 'two threes' or 'three fours'. Pupils who do not understand the vocabulary of multiplication will demonstrate their lack of understanding by showing you five objects (2 and 3) in response to the first request and seven (3 and 4) in response to the second.

1. Build up pupils' understanding gradually, for example by making groups of three objects and saying: *Here's 3. Here's another 3, that's two 3s all together. This is another group of 3, so now we've got three 3s. What must I do to have four 3s?* etc.

2. Focus on the grouping. Let pupils start by simply making the groups distinct, without any special pattern. After a while, if children do not do it for themselves, show pupils how to arrange the objects into rectangular arrays, with rows and columns lined up.

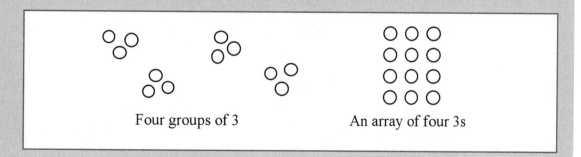

Four groups of 3   An array of four 3s

3. Focus on the total amount. Ask how many counters are in the arrays you have asked them to make. Insist that pupils count in steps to find the total, not in ones.

   Later, ask pupils to predict, or guess, how many counters will be needed to make a particular array, say four 3s or six 2s. Pupils make the array only after they have committed themselves to a guess, and check their answer by counting in steps of at least two, not in ones.

4. Make up little scenarios to turn the arrays into a 'story' or word problem. For example, for the array shown above, you could pretend that each counter represents the plate you eat off at a meal, so the top row shows breakfast, lunch and supper on one day, and the next row represents breakfast, lunch and supper on the next day, etc., so the whole array gives the answer to the question *How many plates are used in four days?* or *How many meals do you eat in 4 days?* Or you might pretend that each nugget is a sweet from a packet of three, or a pupil in a team, or a wheel on a tricycle, etc. Model a few story word problems, then have the pupils make up their own about everyday situations involving small numbers. Some children may need a scribe to record their stories.

 Activity

Connect division to multiplication from the very beginning

In the activities above, the pupils have been introduced to vocabulary such as 'four 3s' without necessarily being told that this is the vocabulary of multiplication. In the same way, introduce division questions without telling the pupils that this is what they are doing.

For example, ask pupils questions such as *If we want to sort 12 counters into groups of three, how many groups will there be?* or, *Let's pretend that these nuggets are balloons and that we're preparing party bags and putting two balloons in each bag. How many bags can we fill with these eight balloons? What if we had 16 balloons?* Or, using the very common sharing model of division, *Say these buttons were made of chocolate and we want to share this chocolate fairly between X people,* etc. When pupils use concrete materials to illustrate these problems, or to help themselves solve these problems, encourage the pupils to organise the materials into rectangular arrays, as shown above.

Activity

Illustrate simple word problems

Both the previous activities involve pupils inventing stories, or word problems, to match arrays that have been built out of concrete materials. Write some of the stories down, including both multiplication problems and division problems, and bring them out at a later lesson without the concrete material.

Read a batch of problems to a group of pupils. Encourage each pupil to illustrate the word problems with sketches or simple drawings, i.e. drawings that do not include any unnecessary detail or decoration. Pupils are often surprised to see that their drawings not only illustrate the question but also provide the answer.

This activity highlights the relationship between multiplication and division because pupils find that there is no difference between the type of sketches that illustrate multiplication and those that illustrate division scenarios.

 Activity

Use Cuisenaire rods to show that multiplication is commutative

This activity is suggested by Prof. Sharma, who writes about it in detail in two of his 1980 *Math Notebook* articles and also demonstrates it in his more recent teaching videos and DVDs. The activity promotes the *area model of multiplication*.

Pupils should repeat the activity with other small rectangles of various numbers of rods.

Step 1

Start with small groups of small numbers, echoing the earlier activities where pupils organised nuggets into arrays, e.g. four 3s, two 5s. Ask pupils now to make these quantities out of Cuisenaire rods. Have pupils arrange the rods into rectangles, like those shown here. Explain to pupils that before we can 'read' these multiplications in terms of numbers, we must agree on a convention about reading the rectangular arrays.

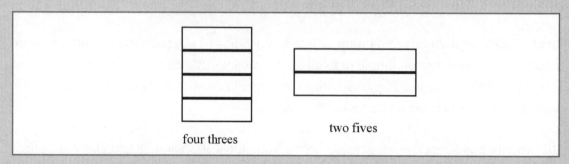

four threes

two fives

The convention that Sharma uses is that the times table is shown by the horizontal length, so that in the figures above the rectangle made of light green rods is part of the 3 times table, and the one made of yellow rods is part of the 5 times table. This means that we 'read' the rectangles first along the vertical and then along the horizontal.

Step 2

After making a rectangle such as 4 × 3, tell pupils that the answer to the multiplication question 4 × 3 lies in the surface area of the rectangle. If necessary, make another rectangle of the same dimensions out of single unit cubes that the pupils can count to prove this fact. Now demonstrate how to read rectangles as multiplication: point to the relevant sides when saying the numbers 4 times 3, and then stroke the surface as you say the solution, *12*. Next have pupils make 3 × 4. This new rectangle must be made of three purple rods. Rotate the rectangle one quarter turn in either direction and place it on top of the light green rectangle. It is, of course, an exact fit. Have pupils read this new rectangle, while pointing to the relevant sides during the question *3 × 4*, and using the palm of their hand on the surface area while giving the answer *12*.

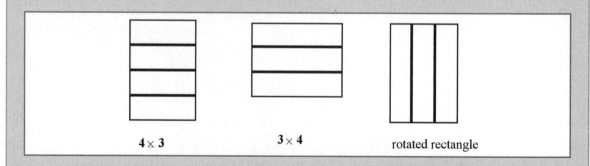

4 × 3

3 × 4

rotated rectangle

Pupils should repeat the activity with other small rectangles of various numbers of rods.

Activities

Use Cuisenaire rods to connect multiplication and division

1. Have pupils make the same kinds of rectangular arrays out of rods as in the previous activity. Demonstrate how to read the rectangle as a division problem. For example, in the 4 × 3 rectangle, use the flat of your hand on the surface while saying *12 can be built from 4* (on the word 'four' point to the vertical side of the rectangle) *threes* (point horizontally along the top of the rectangle), *so 12 divided by 4 is 3, and 12 divided by 3 is 4.* Give pupils lots of practice in making pairs of equivalent rectangles and in reading each rectangle aloud both as a multiplication and as a division.

2. Pupils record multiplication or division facts as rectangles drawn or shaded on squared paper. Squares of 1 cm are best, to match the dimensions of the Cuisenaire rods. Either of the examples below can be used to record either of the multiplication expressions 3 × 4 or 4 × 3, or either of the divisions expressions 12 ÷ 4 or 12 ÷ 3.

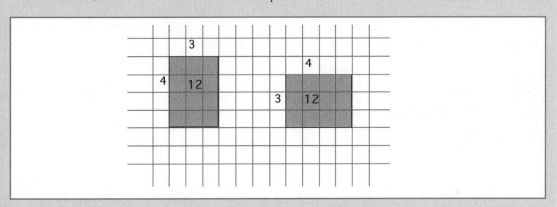

3. Pupils can record the same family of facts as equations in digits:

   3 × 4 = 12   4 × 3 = 12   12 ÷ 3 = 4   12 ÷ 4 = 3

4. Give pupils enough practice so that they can 'see' both possible rectangles whatever the orientation, and will accept that a rectangle made of three black rods, for example, can represent both 3 × 7 and 7 × 3. If they see 3 columns of 7 (with the black rods arranged vertically) they can, with practice, switch in their minds to imagining 7 rows of 3 (with the 3s arranged horizontally).

5. In terms of Cuisenaire rods, division problems can be 'translated' like this: *12 ÷ 3 means that you have to make a rectangle with an area of 12. One side of the rectangle must be 3. The answer will be the other side of the rectangle, along the top.* Having the answer along the top of the rectangle will connect it, later, with the short-division written notation.

   Once the pupils have solved this problem, dismantle the rectangle and lay the rods end to end, against rods that measure 12 units in length (i.e. an orange and a red). Tell pupils that another way of 'translating' the problem is: *How many 3s in 12?*

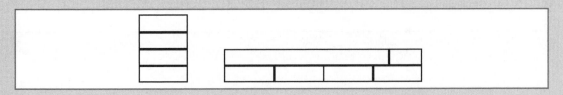

Activity

Connect step-counting (repeated addition) with multiplication

Step 1

Set out ten bases in a row, for example ten squares of paper, or saucers, or shallow trays. Leave a larger gap between the fifth and sixth base.

Step 2

Put two objects on each, for example two glass nuggets or beads, saying: *one two, two twos, three twos, four twos,* etc.

Step 3

Go back to the beginning and announce that now you are finding out how many there are in total, or *how much is ten twos.* Step-count aloud as you point to each group: *two, four, six, eight,* etc.

Pupils should copy your actions and words, until they can carry out all three steps of the activity for themselves.

Instead of the language 'three twos' or 'four twos', you can sometimes substitute 'three groups of two', 'four sets of two', etc. But never use the words 'lots of two', because most children interpret 'lots' as 'a large amount' (as in 'lots and lots of . . .'). Similarly, the word 'times' has no meaning for young children and must be introduced with care.

Repeat the activity for the 5 times table. Arrange the five objects in the familiar spot pattern, to minimise counting and recounting, and to emphasise at the step-counting stage exactly how much is being added at each step.

On another occasion, repeat the activity with a red Cuisenaire rod on each base for the 2 times table and a yellow rod on each base for the 5 times tables. Step-counting in twos and fives must be done without using fingers or counting in ones.

Repeat the activity with an orange Cuisenaire rod on each base for the 10 times table.

Once or twice, have pupils set out 20 bases, with a gap after every five, and step-count in twos, fives or tens. It is important to let pupils set up and complete the whole activity themselves, so that they can internalise the connection between the counting out of the bases and step-counting the total amounts.

 Activity

Step-count one or two steps from various tables facts

Step 1

Set out ten bases, as for the previous activity. Put a red, yellow or orange Cuisenaire rod on each base, depending on which multiplication table you are examining.

Step 2

Take a large sheet of paper and cover some of the bases from the right. From that position, move the paper one step in either direction. For example, cover all the bases except the four at the left. Ask the pupil the value of all the rods they see. Pupils are allowed to step-count to find the answer, e.g. *five, ten, fifteen, twenty*, but may not count in ones.

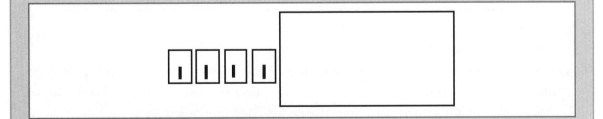

Step 3

Move the paper one place to the right, so that now five bases are showing. Pupils must use their previous answer to tell you the new total; they may not start the step-count from the beginning again. Move the paper back, and ask the pupils to remind themselves how much are four fives, before moving the paper to the left leaving only three bases showing. Again, the aim of the activity is that pupils use their previous answer to find the new total.

Step 4

After practising this activity a few times, it should be possible to use empty bases, with the pupils imagining an amount on each base, at which point you can extend the activity to tables other than 2, 5 and 10. You can photocopy and laminate a page like the example below. Choose any base and write down what multiplication fact it represents. Use a cover sheet to hide the rest of the bases to the right, moving the sheet one base to the left or to the right, as described above, to give pupils practice in working out one step more or one step less than the written product.

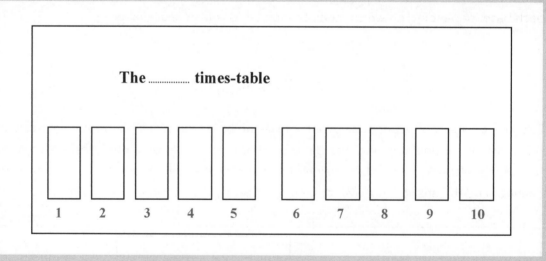

For example, working in the 4 times table, write 32 above the eighth box and say: *Imagine groups of four. These eight bases would total 32, because I know that 8 × 4 = 32*. Move the cover sheet to the left and ask pupils to calculate *one four less than 8 × 4*.

Note that the object of this activity is not to get pupils to learn their tables, but to step-count one or two steps, up or down, from a given or known multiplication fact.

Activity

Practise mental step-counting from given tables facts

Earlier activities recommend that pupils count up and down, at first with the support of concrete materials in ones, later in larger regular steps. Multiplication requires pupils to step-count in groups of various sizes. However, pupils who have difficulties with arithmetic cannot be expected to learn the steps of every multiplication table by heart. Instead, pupils should understand that step-counting is really repeated addition, and many need reminding of how best to deal with addition: *not* by counting in ones, but by adding in chunks along a number line (either on paper or in their mind's eye) and bridging through 10 if necessary.

To practise step-counting in fives, allow pupils to use the number line method of addition, if necessary, until they notice the strong pattern that allows them to step-count mentally, from any starting point that is a multiple of 5. Pupils can be asked to practise quite long sequences of step-counts, both up and down, in ones, twos, fives, and tens, without any concrete or visual supporting materials.

The larger numbers, 9, 8, 7 and 6, are hard, because they all require additions that include bridging through 10. Step-counting in threes and fours may also be difficult for some pupils. To practise these additions, remind pupils of how to use a number line for addition and for bridging through 10, and set them problems that require only one step to be added to a tables product. For example, 18 + 3, 28 + 4, 12 + 6, 18 + 9, 36 + 6, 16 + 8, 35 + 7.

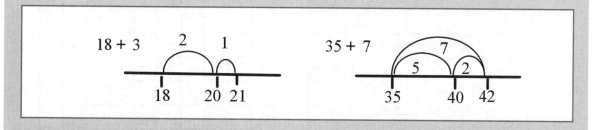

Pupils may choose to record the bridging through 10 in either of the ways shown above, i.e. as two cumulative jumps, or as one jump subdivided into two.

After pupils have done a few additions of this sort on paper, hide their work and have them repeat the steps to the solution on an imaginary number line in their mind's eye. On later occasions, challenge pupils to try two consecutive tables steps on an imaginary number line.

The aim of this activity is to get pupils to the stage of being able to add one or two steps of a tables sequence mentally, even when it involves bridging through 10.

Activities

Make times tables patterns on a 100-square

1. Use a shallow cardboard tray measuring 10 cm x 10 cm (see CD 💿 for net). From left to right, and from the top down, have pupils make the pattern of the 2 times table in the tray. The result will be neat but boring: the whole tray will be filled with red rods (you will need more than one box of rods). The same exercise for the 5 times table and the 10 times table will produce similarly dull and uniformly coloured results.

Try the same exercise for the pattern of the 3 times table. Pupils will be able to fit three light-green rods along the top, but will have to split the next rod into 1 + 2 in order to fit it into the tray. At the end of the next row a rod will have to be split again, but this time the same two components will be used in the reverse order. As pupils fill more and more of the tray, the pattern begins to emerge and pupils can predict what will happen. Pupils also get to see that the number 3 can only be split in one way: 1 + 2 or 2 + 1. Once it fills the tray, the pattern is striking and memorable.

Pupils will benefit from repeating the activity for other numbers. The times table pattern for 6, for example, reveals that the number 6 is only ever split in one way: 2 + 4 or 4 + 2. Knowing this will make pupils more confident when trying to derive new tables facts from known facts, which is what dyscalculic pupils need to learn to do.

The 3 times table made of Cuisenaire rods in a 10 × 10 tray

The pattern of the 3 times table shown by shading on a 100-square

2. A slightly different way of seeing the times tables patterns is to get pupils to shade squares on a numbered paper 100-square. For example, shading every third or ninth number reveals a strong diagonal, while shading every second, fifth or tenth produces unbroken vertical lines.

Encourage pupils to make connections between the patterns made by the 2 and 4 times table, the patterns made by the 3 and 6 times tables, and between the patterns of the 3, 6 and 9 times tables. Point out to your pupils that the 7 times table does not make a strong pattern, which is precisely what makes it such a difficult times table to learn.

 Activities

Make times tables patterns on number lines

These activities target the multiplication tables of the numbers above 5.

1. Give pupils a 'skeleton' of a multiplication table on a number line (see below, and CD). A skeleton is nothing more than a line starting at zero on which ten equal jumps are drawn. Show clearly where the half-way point lies.

   Have pupils fill in all the appropriate numbers for a chosen times table, e.g. 6 ×. Discuss with pupils what they have noticed. You want them to notice that there are only four occasions where bridging through 10 is necessary, and that on each of those occasions the 6 is split in the same way: 4 + 2 (or 2 + 4). You also want them to notice that because 6 is an even number, all the numbers they have labelled on the number line are also even numbers. You can connect this fact to the way 6 is split, since any other way of splitting 6 into components requires odd numbers to be used. (See also the earlier activity on making times tables patterns with Cuisenaire rods.)

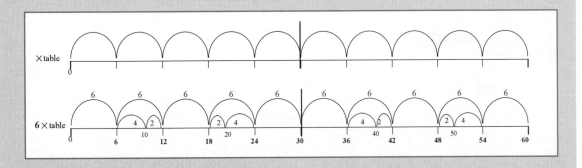

2. Repeat the activity for other multiplication tables. Point out to pupils that the pattern is symmetrical for all multiplication tables at the half-way point of the 10-step table: folding the number line in the middle highlights the fact that the pattern of whole jumps and bridging jumps in the first half of the table is a mirror image of those in the second half of the multiplication table.

The page of skeleton tables on the CD can be laminated and used for pupils to explore the number line patterns of the 6, 7, 8 and 9 times tables.

Activities

Double means 'multiply by 2'

1. Pupils have already done lots of work on doubling (see activities in earlier sections), but now need to connect that knowledge to times table and multiplication work. Give lots of practice in doubling and halving, making a point of using the terms 'multiply' and 'divide' when asking the questions and the signs '×' and '÷' when recording the work.

   Using a mirror can help pupils understand that doubling is not the same as adding, even though the solution to a doubling question can be achieved by adding. Use the vocabulary 'twice as much' and 'twice as many' alongside 'multiply by 2'.

2. Use mirrors together with counters or rods, or drawings with clear mirror lines of symmetry, to show pupils that 'double and double again' is the same as '4 times' a number. This second activity reinforces the idea that doubling means multiplication, not addition.

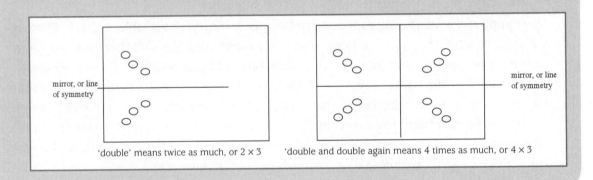

'double' means twice as much, or 2 × 3   'double and double again means 4 times as much, or 4 × 3

 Activity

× 5 is half of × 10

Step 1

Pupils should know the answer to 10 times any number, and they should also know how to make the appropriate rectangle out of Cuisenaire rods to illustrate the area model of multiplication (see Section 3 and earlier activities in this section).

Show pupils how halving any array or rectangle that is made of 10 times a number, would create two new rectangles in which one side is 5 units, i.e. each new rectangular array illustrates a fact from the 5 times table. If pupils choose to make their rectangle out of orange rods, they can either imagine a saw slicing each orange rod in half, or physically remake the rectangle by substituting two yellow rods for every orange one.

Have pupils repeat this activity with other numbers, until they have entirely convinced themselves that 5 times a number is always half of 10 times the number.

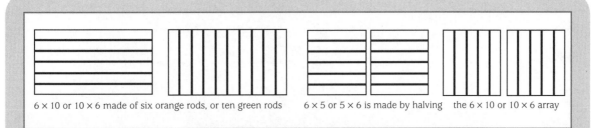

6 × 10 or 10 × 6 made of six orange rods, or ten green rods   6 × 5 or 5 × 6 is made by halving   the 6 × 10 or 10 × 6 array

Step 2

Give pupils written practice of finding 5 times a number. At first, ask pupils to write the intermediate step, as in the example below. Noting the intermediate fact helps pupils focus on which number needs manipulating, which is especially useful in situations where the 5 sometimes appears before and sometimes after the multiplication sign.

8×5 = half of __80__ = _____

5×6 = half of _____ = _____

12×5 = half of _____ = _____

5×20 = half of _____ = _____   etc.

Step 3

Show pupils how to reduce the amount of writing by substituting the fraction '$\frac{1}{2}$' for the word 'half' and the multiplication sign '×' for the word 'of'. Pupils will find this knowledge (i.e. half of ... = $\frac{1}{2} \times$ ...) very useful later, both when solving word problems and when working with fractions.

 Activity

Find all the steps of any times table by reasoning from key facts

Dorian Yeo, in her 2003 book *Dyslexia, Dyspraxia and Mathematics*, calls this the 'universal strategy' for all times tables. Pupils feel reassured to know that the demands on their memory will be limited to a few key facts, and that they will not have to remember different strategies for each different multiplication table.

Show pupils that a multiplication table is a string of ten facts:

$1 \times$

$2 \times$

3 ×

4 ×

5 ×

6 ×

7 ×

8 ×

9 ×

10 ×

The ten basic steps should be presented vertically, as shown above. Have pupils highlight the numbers 5 and 10, and remind pupils of the previous activity where they learned and practised how to find these two key facts.

Work though all the times tables, other than 1, 2, 5 and 10, starting with the 3s. Pupils immediately know the answers to 1 × 3 (the same number), 2 × 3 (double the number), and the key facts 10 × 3 and 5 × 3 (from the previous activity). They can now use their step-counting techniques to fill in all the blanks: 3 × 3 is one step above the double fact, 4 × 3 is either one further step, or double 3 and double again. 6 × 3 is one step more than 5 × 3 (or double 3 × 3), and 9 × 3 is one step less than 10 × 3. This leaves two empty spaces, the 7× and 8×, always the hardest steps of any times table. Pupils usually choose to calculate 7× in two steps from 5×. There are three choices for 8×: three steps up from 5×, or two steps back from 10× (the least popular and often the least accurate choice), or double the 4× fact (i.e. double and double again to get the 4× fact, then double yet again). Pupils should be allowed to choose their favourite strategy for 8×, but should be encouraged to stick to the same chosen strategy for all the tables.

A good idea, when working on this reasoning technique with pupils, is to ask for answers to be given orally only, and not to allow pupils to record the answers every time they practise a table. Ask the questions in a random sequence, too. If pupils find the answers in order, they will only add one step from the answer before, instead of practising finding new facts from known key facts. Encourage pupils to talk aloud through their reasoning. For example, if asked 9 × 3, the pupil might say: *9 times 3, that's one 3 less than 10 × 3, so 3 less than 30, which is 27.*

A single laminated sheet of the vertical presentation on the previous page can be used for practising all the tables, using a dry-wipe pen for ticking or crossing off correct answers. It can be sent home for extra practice, instead of written homework, to allow pupils to do all their thinking aloud without embarrassment and without disturbing other pupils. However, parents must be told that the aim of the homework is for pupils to practise reasoning efficiently from key facts. The actual answers are of only secondary importance, so working out the sequence in order, or calculating by counting in ones, would defeat the purpose of the exercise.

Note that pupils with dyscalculia will probably never be able to remember their times tables facts, however many times they practise them. The aim of these activities, therefore, is for pupils to realise that only a few crucial facts have to be memorised, and that new facts can be derived by logic.

 Activity

× 9 is almost × 10

The 9 times table is an easy one to learn for children who are familiar with Cuisenaire rods and with the area model of multiplication. For example, for 9 × 4, make a rectangle of 10 × 4 and show where an imaginary saw could chop off one unit from the end of every 10-rod. The solution to 9 × 4 is therefore clearly seen to be 40 – 4, which those knowing their complement facts can quickly answer.

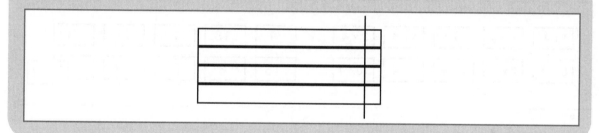

 # Games
to practise individual times tables
using self-correcting cards

The cheapest and most versatile resource for practising individual times tables is a set of self-correcting cards, with the questions shown on one side and the corresponding answers on the back. Cards like this can be bought, or they can be made by pupils or teachers (in which case, use a different colour of card for different times tables).

Game 1.

Use the cards for learning and revision. The pupil tries to answer all the questions, first in order, then shuffled, against the clock, or in a race with another pupil.

Game 2.

As above, but with the cards arranged so that the answers are face up. The pupil, knowing which times table is being practised, must supply the question. Allow pupils to phrase the question in either of two ways, e.g. for a card showing 15, both 3 × 5 and 5 × 3 are correct, whether it is the 5 times table or the 3 times table that is being practised.

Variation:

The pupil expresses the table fact as a division, e.g. 15 ÷ 3 = 5 or 15 ÷ 5 = 3.

Game 3.

Match the questions to the answer. Use one set of cards laid out on a table in an array with the questions face up, as shown below on the left. At first the cards are laid out in order, later in a random order. The pupil uses a second, shuffled, set of cards with the answers face up. The pupil must place each card in turn onto the matching card as quickly as possible. Pupils can play this against the clock, or race alongside other pupils with their own sets and arrays of cards.

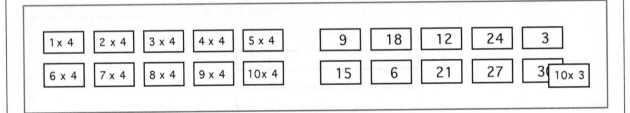

Variation:

Play in reverse, with the pupil matching the answers to the questions, as shown above on the right.

Game 4.

Two pupils have two or more sets of cards each, for the same times table. One pupil's cards are arranged with the questions face up and other pupil's cards are arranged with the answers face up. The cards are shuffled and the pupils play Snap.

Game
Don't Walk If You Can Take the Bus

This is a game for two or more players. Players make the game board before play starts.

Teaching points:

- ◆ The game practises any desired multiplication table.
- ◆ It teaches players to derive new facts from the key tables of 2 ×, 5 × and 10 ×.

Equipment needed:

◆ Cuisenaire rods.

◆ 1 cm squared paper for the game board.

◆ A pawn or token.

◆ Four 'bus stops' (lolly sticks or toothpicks stuck in Blu-Tack).

◆ A 1–10 die.

Rules:

Players take ten rods to match the multiplication table they are practising. The rods are placed end to end on the squared paper. Pupils draw an arrow pointing to the end of each rod, and label each arrow with the question of the multiplication table sequence, but not the answer. The example below, for the 6 times table, would be made of dark-green rods and labelled as shown. Pupils erect the 'bus stops' by sticking them into a blob of Blu-Tack at the end of the first, second, fifth and tenth (final) rod.

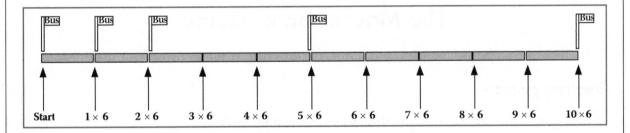

Put the pawn on the start arrow at the beginning of every turn. Players take turns to throw the die and move the pawn to the arrow that matches the throw. On each turn, the player may take one bus journey of either 1, 2, 3 or 4 stops, and may then need to 'walk' the pawn a little further, in either direction, to reach the required spot. On arrival, the player must answer the times tables question correctly. If the answer is wrong, the pawn has to go back to the nearest 'bus stop' and be 'walked' again, while the player tries to get the step-counting right. A scorer keeps a tally score of the number of rods, i.e. times tables steps, that each player 'walks' on each turn. The scoring, in which the lowest score wins, gives players an incentive to minimise the number of steps of reasoning, and to step-count carefully from the nearest key fact.

For example, a player who throws 9 on the die and chooses to take the bus to 10 and walk back will score an excellent 1, whereas a player who chooses to take the bus to 5 and walk forwards will score 4, and if the answer is not correct until after a second try the score will go up to 8.

The winner is the player with the lowest score after, say, 5 minutes.

Variation:

For younger players working on the early tables (3 ×, 4 × and 5 ×), the board can be made to show dot patterns instead of rods. In this case, draw a wide 'road' on plain paper, divide it into ten equal stretches, and draw one dot pattern in each section. The example overleaf shows what a game for the 4 times table would look like.

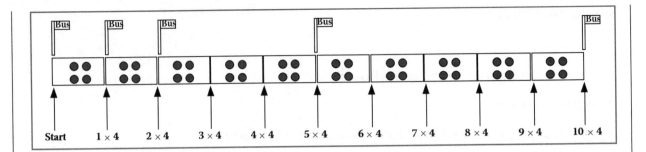

Tip:

Whichever variation the pupils are playing, the scorer should be someone who knows the correct answers and who will insist that the reasoning from the key fact is achieved by step-counting and bridging, not by counting in ones.

Game

The Mouse Tables Game

This lovely game, for two players (and a mouse), was taught to me by Laura Thompson.

Teaching points:

◆ The game gives practice in any desired multiplication table.

◆ It gives practice in step-counting and in matching answers to multiplication questions.

◆ It does not put any time pressure on players, and therefore encourages logical thinking.

◆ It extends the reasoning technique to two steps beyond the normal tables limit, i.e. to the 12 times table.

Equipment needed:

◆ A paper template, like the one shown on the next page. It should first be enlarged to A4 for younger children or A5 for older players.

◆ Twelve laminated cards small enough for all of them to fit onto the board.

◆ A dry-wipe pen.

◆ A small finger puppet in the shape of a mouse, of just the right size to contain one card (or an envelope with a picture of a mouse on it).

Rules:

Players share the same board and write in each box the table that's being practised, after the multiplication sign. The two players step-count aloud and write one product on each of the 12 laminated answer cards, using the dry-wipe pen. The cards are turned face down and mixed up. One card at random is taken and put, still face down, inside the mouse finger-puppet. Players now take turns to pick up any card, read the number and match it to the question, using it to cover the appropriate box as soon as their opponent agrees that they have matched correctly. Play proceeds until nine boxes have been covered and only two cards remain to be placed (remember, there is another card in the mouse). Both players must now pause and guess what number the mouse is hiding. They have a one in three chance of guessing correctly (assuming they can work out the right answers to the three remaining questions). The players write their guess on a piece of scrap paper, and play on. The game can end in a draw, if players do not consult when writing their prediction. If neither player guesses correctly, the mouse is deemed to have won.

Tips:

Do not rush pupils: the scoring system of this game is deliberately designed to take the focus off the speed with which pupils must find a tables fact, in order to encourage reasoning and also in order to promote the idea that accuracy is more important than speed.

Do not be tempted to provide the pupils with ready-prepared answer cards: the act of step-counting and physically writing the multiples before the game can start is an important part of the learning experience. If you copy and laminate a board like the one shown below, it can be used and reused for any table.

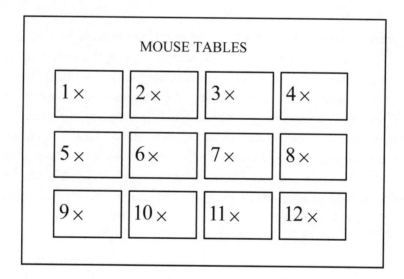

Variation:

Adapt the game for division. The board would then be made of 12 empty rectangles, and the 12 answer cards will each show a number from 1 to 12. Before play, pupils start by step-counting aloud and writing the first 12 steps of the count on the board, with one multiple written in each rectangle and with each multiple being followed by a division sign. The multiples can sometimes be written in ascending or descending order on the board, and sometimes mixed up in no particular order. The number of the times table that is being practised should be written after each division sign.

Activity

Construct a multiplication grid

Tables squares can be bought commercially, and there is a particularly useful version available in foldable plastic. All dyscalculic pupils should be allowed to use tables squares when the problems they are working on are not primarily designed to practise multiplication facts.

In this activity pupils make their own multiplication grid, so that they really understand what the numbers represent and how they relate to each other.

Step 1

Make an empty grid on paper with 1 cm squares, by marking out a 10 cm × 10 cm square and labelling each column and each row from 1 to 10.

Step 2

Start with any easy multiplication with which the pupils are already familiar, e.g. 2 × 3. Use Cuisenaire rods to build the multiplication as a rectangle (using the area model of multiplication, as in earlier activities). Place the light green rectangle on the multiplication grid at the top left-hand corner. Use a large L-shaped piece of card, as shown below, to isolate the rectangle. Show pupils how to use the grid labelling to 'read' the multiplication as both 3 × 2 and 2 × 3. Remove the rods, but leave the L-shaped guide in place. The answer to the multiplication, which the pupil already knows to be 6, can be clearly seen in the six empty squares that the L-shape has isolated. Pupils write the number 6 in the 6th square reading from left to right and top to bottom, which is also, of course, the square where the column and row labelled 3 and 2 intersect.

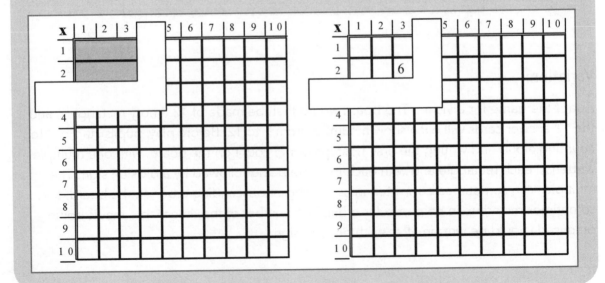

Step 3

Rotate the rods rectangle and repeat the procedure with the rectangle and the L-shaped guide to find the second position on the grid for the answer 6.

Step 4

Repeat the procedure with rods on the grid for other familiar multiplications. After a while, it should not be necessary for pupils to physically rotate the rectangle in order to find the second position of the multiple. Remind pupils of their earlier work with rods when they explored the commutative property of multiplication. This means that if they know the answer to, say 4×7, they also know the answer to 7×4.

Step 5

Have pupils make all the square numbers out of rods and write the answers on the grid. Pupils should notice the diagonal line produced by these answers, and should also notice that these answers appear only once on the grid, in contrast to all the other numbers which appear in two places, on either side of the newly created diagonal.

Step 6

As soon as they are ready, pupils can dispense with physically making the rectangles out of rods. At this stage, pupils can abandon the 10 cm square, in favour of one on a larger scale that will be much easier to read clearly when filled with a hundred numbers. Many pupils will still find the L-shaped guide useful, especially those with dyspraxia who cannot easily track a straight line by sight alone.

Step 7

Teach pupils how to use the grid for division as well as for multiplication.

Activity

Complete a partially-filled multiplication grid

Although it is very useful for pupils to fill in a whole multiplication grid once or twice, it is also very time-consuming. In order to target particular tables, or the hardest multiplication facts, provide pupils with partially-numbered grids to complete, like those below.

X	1	2	3	4	5	6	7	8	9	10
1	1	2	3	4	5		7	8	9	10
2	2	4	6	8	10		14	16	18	20
3	3	6	9	12	15		21	24	27	30
4	4	8	12	16	20		28	32	36	40
5	5	10	15	20	25		35	40	45	50
6										
7	7	14	21	28	35		49	56	63	70
8	8	16	24	32	40		56	64	72	80
9	9	18	27	36	45		63	72	81	90
10	10	20	30	40	50		70	80	90	100

Partially completed grid for practising the 6 × table

X	1	2	3	4	5	6	7	8	9	10
1	1	2	3	4	5	6	7	8	9	10
2	2	4	6	8	10	12	14	16	18	20
3	3	6	9	12	15				27	30
4	4	8	12	16	20				36	40
5	5	10	15	20	25	30	35	40	45	50
6	6	12			30				54	60
7	7	14			35				63	70
8	8	16			40				72	80
9	9	18	27	36	45	54	63	72	81	90
10	10	20	30	40	50	60	70	80	90	100

Grid for practising the 12 'hardest' tables facts

Game

Multiples from the 1–6 Times Tables

A game for two players.

Teaching points:

◆ The game practises the multiplication tables facts up to 6 × 6.

◆ It provides a way of learning and remembering the meaning of the word 'multiple'.

◆ It reinforces the fact that all even numbers are in the 2 times table (and vice versa).

◆ It helps pupils notice the connection between tables, especially between the 2 times and the 4 times tables, and between the 3 times and the 6 times tables.

◆ It reinforces the relationship between multiplication and division.

Equipment needed:

◆ A playing board with a 6 x 6 grid on which the numbers 1–36 are shown (see CD).

◆ A 6-sided die and counters in two colours, one colour for each player.

Rules:

Players take turns to throw the die and to put one of their own counters on any number on the board that is a multiple of the number shown on the die. The winner is the first player to have four counters in a row.

The Multiples Game
Multiples from the 1 - 6 times tables

1	2	3	4	5	6
7	8	9	10	11	12
13	14	15	16	17	18
19	20	21	22	23	24
25	26	27	28	29	30
31	32	33	34	35	36

RULES   This game is for 2 players
You will need a 1 - 6 die and counters in two colours

Players take turns to throw the die and to put one of their counters on any number that is a multiple of the number shown on the die.   For example, if you throw a 2, cover any multiple of 2, which means any number from the 2 times table, (which also means any even number)

The winner is the first person to get four counters in a row

Activity

Harder mixed tables practice

Because the game above only practises the easier tables facts, this activity is designed to follow on from it and to give practice in the harder tables facts.

Put together two packs of digit cards, each containing only the numbers from 5 to 9. Each pack contains four cards for each of the five numbers. Shuffle both packs and turn them face down.

The pupil picks up one card from each pack and must multiply the numbers by each other, using previously learned reasoning techniques.

This activity can be set up in pairs, with one pupil using a multiplication square, or a calculator, to check the other's answers. Pupils swap roles when the packs have been used up once.

For pupils who find this activity too difficult, you could at first build one of the packs out of all the numbers from 1 to 9.

Game

Factors

A game for two or three players.

Teaching points:

◆ The game gives division practice but without mentioning the word *division*.

◆ It provides a way of learning and remembering the meaning of the word *factor*.

◆ It encourages pupils to notice that some numbers appear in more than one multiplication table.

◆ It shows that although some numbers have more factors than others, this has nothing to do with the magnitude of the number.

◆ It teaches pupils that factors always come in pairs: *two* numbers are multiplied together to get a product.

Equipment needed:

◆ A playing board featuring some multiples of various times tables (two boards are given on the CD 💿 for different levels of difficulty).

◆ A die.

- A token for each player.
- Paper and pencil.
- Rods (or coins) for collecting and scoring.

Rules:

Players takes turns to throw the die and move around the board. When landing on each number, the player writes down all the possible factors except 1 and the number itself. Players accumulate rods (or coins) to match each of the factors they identify. The winner has the most rods (or coins) after all the players have been around the board twice.

Tips:

Do not allow pupils to add up their winnings as they go along, since all scoring is based on addition, whereas the game itself focuses on multiplication and division. If possible, judge the winner by eye without adding to find exact scores.

The game should be played with the teacher as one of the players (but one whose score does not count), to check the pupils' answers and to model for the pupils how to find as many factors as possible for each number.

Use the word *factor* as often as possible when playing this game. However, to avoid muddling pupils, never use the word *multiple* when referring to the numbers on the board. If you must give them a name, call them *products* in this game.

Insist that factors must always come in pairs. For example, pupils recognising an even number may offer 2 as a factor, and could then be prompted, *yes, 2 and what else?*

Activity

Diagrammatic practice of the area model of multiplication

Have pupils sketch various rectangles, like the examples below, for practising the area model of multiplication, and for making the connection between multiplication and division. The sketches need have no relationship to the actual size of the numbers.

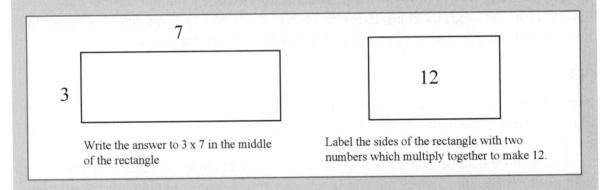

Write the answer to 3 x 7 in the middle of the rectangle

Label the sides of the rectangle with two numbers which multiply together to make 12.

Use an empty template, like the one provided on the CD 💿 to make a page full of problems for pupils to solve or for pupils to make up for each other to solve.

A bonus of using the area model of multiplication, and of using the term explicitly with pupils, is that it eliminates later confusion between the terms *area* and *perimeter*.

 Activity

Use rectangle sketches to help derive new multiplication facts

This activity encourages pupils to practise reasoning from known facts that are beyond the times tables facts. For example, given the fact that 15 × 6 is 90, how can we use that knowledge to find 7 × 15? Most pupils at this stage would understand that something must be added to 90, but many would be unsure whether to add a group of 15 or a group of 6.

Putting the information on a sketch is a quick way to clarify one's thinking. The rectangle shows 15 times 6, and as soon as the rectangle is altered to show 7 times 15, the pupil can see that one 'slice' 15 long, or one group of 15, must be added.

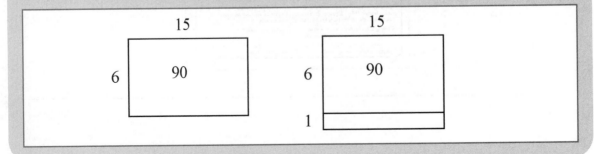

Give pupils practice, as in the worksheet extract below. Encourage pupils to sketch a rectangle for each problem, and then to turn their paper over and visualise the sketch in their mind. Once pupils are very familiar with the technique, they should try to answer these types of questions mentally.

Here are four sample questions extracted from a worksheet:

$6 \times 10 = 60,$ *so* $6 \times 12 =$

$10 \times 12 = 120,$ *so* $11 \times 12 =$

$12 \times 5 = 60,$ *so* $13 \times 5 =$

$9 \times 15 = 135,$ *so* $9 \times 16 =$

 ## Activities

Change the shape of the multiplication rectangle

Use large cubes to start off these activities: 1 cm cubes are too fiddly, but cubes of about three times the size are ideal. (Mine are made of foam and called 'DIME Cubes'.)

1. Take 12 cubes and have pupils arrange them into a rectangle representing a multiplication fact of their choice. The possibilities are: 3×4, 2×6 or 1×12. Show pupils how they can change the shape of their rectangle by halving one side and moving half the rectangle so as to double the other side. For example, a 2×6 rectangle can become a 4×3 rectangle, and vice versa.

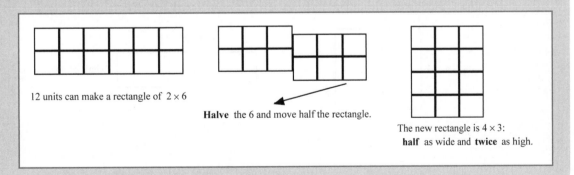

12 units can make a rectangle of 2×6

Halve the 6 and move half the rectangle.

The new rectangle is 4×3: **half** as wide and **twice** as high.

Similarly, for a 1 × 12 shape, the rectangle can be halved along the 12-unit side and regrouped to create a new rectangle measuring 2 × 6. Have pupils practise transforming one shape of rectangle into another, while explaining aloud exactly what is happening. Pupils should read each newly formed rectangle as a multiplication, just as they learned to do during earlier activities with Cuisenaire rods.

2. Have pupils explore other small rectangles, made of an even number of cubes, in the same way. Ask pupil why there are three possible shapes for 12 (see above) but only two possible shapes for 4 or 14. Use the word factor and encourage pupils also use the term.

3. Extend the above activity to numbers with factors other than 2. For example, ask pupils how many different shapes of rectangles can be made out of 9 cubes? [Answer: two.] Can we transform one rectangle into the other by halving and doubling, as before? [Answer: no, but we can use the same principle, with 3 as our factor. This time, one side is split into thirds and the other side is tripled.] How many shapes of rectangle will 18 produce? [Answer: three.] Have pupils practise transforming each rectangle into another and encourage them to explain what is happening, in their own words.

4. Ask pupils how many possible shapes there are for 5 or 7. [Answer: one.] This is a good opportunity to talk about prime numbers and to explore other small primes. In terms of the rectangular array that models multiplication, a prime number is a number that can only be formed into a long thin rectangle, 1 unit high (and more than 1 unit wide).

5. Use diagrammatic sketches to illustrate all the same rectangles as in the steps above, this time without the concrete materials being present. For example, sketch a rough square, labelling the two sides 4 and the central area 16. Sketch a second rectangle, longer and thinner than the square (but there is no need to try and keep to scale) and label the centre 16. Ask pupils what the dimensions of the sides will now be if one side is doubled and the other side is halved. Let pupils practise more of these kinds of manipulations on paper.

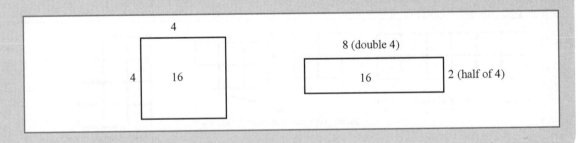

Game
Areas on a Grid

This is a game for two players.

Teaching points:

◆ This is a game of strategy.

◆ The game relates multiplication and division through the area model.

◆ It draws pupils' attention to the fact that some multiples appear in more than one times table.

Equipment needed:

◆ Squared paper and pencils.

◆ A die on which the following numbers are shown: 6, 8, 12, 16, 18 and 24 (write on a blank die or use stickers over the faces of an ordinary die).

Rules:

Each player marks out for themselves a 10 × 10 grid on squared paper. Players take it in turns to throw the die and to shade in a rectangle of the area of the number thrown, on their own grid. Pupils may choose any size of rectangle with the required area, the aim being to fit as many rectangles as possible into the grid. For example, a throw of 6 can be represented by a rectangle measuring either 1 × 6 or 2 × 3. The first player who cannot fit a new rectangle into the remaining space on his/her grid loses the game. (Players should take turns to be the first player to start.)

Variation:

Both players use the same grid, which measures 12 × 12 squares. Players take turns to start a game. Players take turns to throw the die and to shade a rectangle on the shared grid. The first person who cannot find space on the grid to shade a new rectangle loses the game.

Suggestions for further reading

Brian Butterworth and Dorian Yeo (2004) *Dyscalculia Guidance*, nferNelson.

Department for Education and Skills (2001) *Guidance to Support Pupils with Dyslexia and Dyscalculia*, Ref. 0512/2001. London: DfES.

Eva Grauberg (1998) *Elementary Mathematics and Language Difficulties*, Whurr.

Derek Haylock (1995, new edn 2006) *Mathematics Explained for Primary Teachers*, Paul Chapman.

Martin Hughes (1986) *Children and Number: Difficulties in Learning Mathematics*, Basil Blackwell.

Tim Miles and Elaine Miles (eds) (1992, new edn 2004) *Dyslexia and Mathematics*, Routledge.

Mahesh Sharma (1980–1993) *Math Notebook*, Center for Teaching/Learning of Mathematics, Framingham, Mass. (Professor Sharma's publications, videos and DVDs are available in the UK from Berkshire Mathematics.)

Mahesh Sharma (1980) Multiplication, *Math Notebook*, vol. 1, nos 9–10. Centre for Teaching/Learning Mathematics, Framingham, Mass.

Mahesh Sharma (1993) Cuisenaire rods and mathematics teaching, *Math Notebook*, vol.10, nos 3–4. Centre for Teaching/Learning Mathematics, Framingham, Mass.

Ian Thompson (ed.) (1997) *Teaching and Learning Early Number*, Open University Press.

Ian Thompson (ed.) (1999) *Issues in Teaching Numeracy in Primary Schools*, Open University Press.

Ian Thompson (ed.) (2003) *Enhancing Primary Mathematics Teaching*, Open University Press.

Dorian Yeo (2003) *Dyslexia, Dyspraxia and Mathematics*, Whurr.

Index

abacus 38–9, 43–4, 60–1, 72, 82
  Slavonic 43–4, 60–1
  spike 38–9, 72, 82
abstract thinking xvi, 2–3, 9, 13, 33, 35–6, 71–2, 74, 76, 82, 85–6, 104
addition 1–5, 9, 11–12, 14–15, 17–18, 22, 26–33, 35–69, 74, 79, 83, 85–6, 88–9, 95–6, 104, 110, 113, 116, 129–30
  in columns 56–8
  in relation to subtraction 11–12, 22, 27–9, 30–1, 37, 41, 46, 53–4, 104
ADHD xix
area 103, 108, 130, 133
area model, see multiplication
array 103, 105–9, 116–7, 120, 132

base ten materials 33–4, 38, 73, 77–80, 85, 89, 92, 95, 99–100, see also Dienes
Basic 8 strategies 37, 68–9
bead strings 2, 5, 16–17, 21, 32, 42–5, 60, Appendix
bridging technique 17, 35, 37, 47–56, 63, 68, 97, 103–4, 113, 115, 122
  through five 17
  through ten 35, 37, 47–52, 63, 68, 97, 103–4, 113, 115, 122
  through multiples of ten 47, 51–6, 68, 113, 115, 122

calculator 16, 21, 85–6, 94, 128
cardinal property 2
cards xv, 2–5, 15, 20–1, 37, 46–7, 49, 68, 73, 78, 81, 85–6, 91–5, 98–9, 119–20, 122–3, 128, CD
column arithmetic 56–9, 80
columns for place value 71–7, 79–80, 85–6, 87–93, 99–101, 104
commutative property 4, 50, 57, 107–8, 125
complementary addition 28, 30–1, 35, 37, 46, 53–6, 59, 61, 68–9, 104
complements 17–21, 32–3, 35, 37, 44–56, 59–62, 66, 68–9, 119
  to 10 17–21, 32, 37, 48–51
  to 20 44–5
  to 100 46, 59–62
components 2–3, 10–11, 14, 18, 26, 32–4, 37, 41, 44–5, 48, 57, 60, 66–7, 72, 104, 114–15

concrete materials xvi, 1–2, 4–5, 22, 35–6, 38, 41, 47, 54, 57, 72–4, 76, 78–80, 82, 85–6, 89–90, 92, 95, 99–100, 104, 106, 113, 131–2, Appendix
concrete models xv, 1–2, 5, 35–6, 53–4, 60, 62–3, 72, 76, 104, 124, 131–2, see also multiplication area model
counting 1–2, 5, 7–9, 16–17, 24, 26, 29–33, 35, 37, 42–3, 45, 53–4, 56, 60–2, 69, 72–5, 80, 85, 97, 103–4, 106, 108, 110–13, 118, 121–3
  backwards xvii–xviii, 2, 24, 31, 37, 74
  in ones 1–2, 16–17, 21, 24, 26, 30–2, 35–7, 43, 54, 61, 72, 74, 85, 97, 104, 111, 133, 118, 122
  step counting 33–4, 73–4, 103–4, 106, 110–13, 118, 121–3
  the trap 1, 35
Cuisenaire rods xv, 1–2, 5–8, 10–11, 18, 22, 24–8, 32, 35, 36, 38, 40–1, 45–9, 60, 62–5, 67, 72–8, 80, 85, 103–4, 107–9, 111, 114–17, 119, 121, 124–5, 129, 132
  introduction to xvi, Appendix
  leaflet xvi, 5, CD
  staircase 6, 18, 26, 40, 45, 75–6

decimals 71, 88, 90, 99–101
decomposition 57, 59, 72, 74, 76, 80–1, 95
diagrammatic models xvi, 2, 4, 31, 37, 53, 72, 82, 103–4, 130–2, see also number lines, multiplication area model and rectangles
dice xv, 3, 8–10, 14, 24–5, 27–8, 32–3, 47, 52, 59–63, 73–7, 79–80, 83–86, 94, 96, 121, 127–9, 133
dice patterns 3–4, 10, 21–2, 26, 37, 121, CD
Dienes blocks xv, 25, 36, 39, 45, 54, 59, 72–4, 76–7, 80, 85, 103, Appendix
difference 18, 28, 30–1, 53, 105, 107
direction 31–2, 45, 53, 65, 66–7, 82, 96
directional difficulty xviii
division xv–xvi, 22, 90, 95, 99, 103–33
  as inverse of multiplication 22, 104, 106–7 109, 120, 125, 127, 129–30, 133
  factors 128–9, 132
  sharing or grouping 103–8, 110, 112–13
dot patterns, see dice patterns
doubles 3–4, 10, 22–3, 32, 62–6, 68–9, 116, 118, 131–2
dyslexia xv, xvii–xviii, 3–4, 35, 117
dyspraxia xv, xvii–xviii, 1, 3–4, 25, 117, 125

equal 4, 7, 11–12, 22, 27–8, 41, 45, 53, 73, 103–5,
    115, 121
equations 11–12, 18, 22, 26–7, 39, 41, 80, 109
estimating xvii–xviii, 7, 24–5, 35, 40, 51–2, 104
exchange 8, 49, 71, 73–4, 76, 80

factors, *see* division

game boards CD
Grauberg, Eva 43, 89
grids 19, 105, 124–7, 133

half 22–3, 50, 63–5, 115–17, 131–2
help xvi, 1–3, 4, 6, 12, 17, 26, 30–1, 35–7, 41, 44–5,
    62, 64, 71–2, 75, 77, 89, 103–5, 116–17, 130
hidden quantities 17, 26, 29, 43, 45
hundred-squares 36, 42–3, 46, 76, 83–4, 114, CD

informal recording, *see* notation

jumps 9–10, 47, 49–53, 56, 61, 96–7, 113, 115

language 3, 35, 43, 67, 105, 110, *see also* vocabulary

memory xvii–xviii, 1–2, 35–6, 54, 103, 117, 119
    difficulties xvii–xviii, 1, 54, 103, 119
    long-term xvii–xviii, 1–2, 35–6
    short-term or working xvii–xviii, 1, 36
mental calculation 16–17, 30–1, 33–5, 41, 47, 51,
    54–5, 57–61, 65, 68, 71–2, 85, 96, 103–4, 113,
    131
misconceptions xvi, 1, 71
missing addends 12, 18, 28–9, 46, 53
money xviii, 7–8, 33–4, 59, 61–2, 72, 73–4, 77, 80,
    101, 129
multiplication xv, xvi, 22, 88, 99, 103–33
    area model 103–5, 107–8, 109, 116–17, 119, 124,
    130–3
    in relation to division 22, 99, 104, 106–7 109, 120,
    125, 127, 129–30, 133
    tables 103–33

notation 3, 12, 36, 57–9, 64, 72, 95, 109
    informal recording 3, 12, 36, 57–8, 64, 72, 95
number lines 9–10, 31, 35–7, 39, 44, 47, 49–56, 59,
    61, 63, 96–7, 113, 115
number sense 1, 24, 35, 71–2, 104
number tracks 9, 26, 36, 42–3, 46

ordering, *see* sequencing

partitioning 37, 41, 57–8, 72, 95, 104
patterns xvii–xviii, 2–4, 6, 10–11, 17, 22, 26, 35–8,
    71–2, 75, 78, 87, 100, 103–5, 110, 113–15, 121
place value xv, xvi, 35, 41, 57, 64, 71–101, 104

reasoning strategies 32, 35, 41, 43, 66, 103–5, 107,
    118, 121–3, 128, 130–2
rectangles 26, 45, 49, 65, 103–9, 116, 119, 123–5,
    130–3
rods, *see* Cuisenaire
rounding 42–44, 98–9

sequence xviii, 6–7, 11, 26, 35, 52, 91–2, 100–1, 103,
    113, 118, 120–1, 123
Sharma, Mahesh 5, 11, 13, 75, 91, 107–8
Slavonic abacus, *see* abacus
solitaire games 10, 14–15, 19, 81, 96
spinners 8, 73, 75, 79
staircase, *see* Cuisenaire rods
step counting, *see* counting
subitising xviii, 17, 45
subtraction 1–3, 11–12, 26–32, 35–69, 72, 79, 80–1,
    83, 85–6, 88, 94–5, 104
    in columns 56, 59, 80,
    as complementary addition 30–1, 35, 37, 46, 53–6,
    59, 61, 68–9, 104
    as inverse of addition 11–12, 22, 27–9, 30–1, 37, 41,
    46, 53–4
Sugarman, Ian 77, 85–6

Thompson, Ian 77, 85
Thompson, Laura 122
time xviii, 36
times tables, *see* multiplication
transition 2, 35–6, 54, 72, 82, Appendix

visualising 16, 37–9, 47, 51, 54–5, 61, 63–4, 72, 78,
    103, 113, 131–2
vocabulary 3, 10, 26, 37, 72, 81, 105–6, 116, *see also*
    language

word problems 3, 13, 37, 39, 46, 105–7, 117
worksheets xv, 2, 36, 61, 64, 66, 69, 131, CD
written work xv, 2–3, 12, 36, 39, 56, 58–9, 72, 76,
    87–8, 90–2, 95, 101, 105, 117–18

Yeo, Dorian 3–4, 79, 117

zero 31, 44, 51, 53, 59, 71, 73, 87–9, 91–2, 94, 99,
    101, 115